A practical guide to growing

HEALTHY HOUSE PLANTS

A practical guide to growing

HEALTHY HOUSE PLANTS

Matthew Biggs

CLB

Colour Library Books

CLB 4479
This edition published 1996 by Colour Library Books

Printed and bound in Singapore
ISBN 1-85833-525-6

Half-title page: Bromeliads are becoming increasingly popular with houseplant enthusiasts looking for something 'different'.

Title page: Streptocarpus hybrids are some of the most popular houseplants, producing delightful flowers in shades of white, blue, mauve and pink.

Below: Being neat and compact, African violets are ideal houseplants where space is limited.

Credits
Edited and designed: Ideas into Print
Plant portraits and propagation sequences: Neil Sutherland
Typesetting: Ideas into Print
Production Director: Gerald Hughes
Production: Ruth Arthur, Sally Connolly, Neil Randles, Karen Staff, Jonathan Tickner

MATTHEW BIGGS trained in horticulture at Pershore College and later at The Royal Botanic Gardens, Kew. He worked there as a guide lecturer and staff training officer and won awards for his lectures. For several years, he ran a landscaping and garden maintenance company. His broadcasting career began on London News Radio and he has recorded gardening slots for Radio 5 and made guest appearances on Meridian's *Grass Roots* and the BBC's *Gardeners' Question Time*. He spent five years as one of the presenters of Channel 4 TV's *Garden Club*. Matthew writes regularly for *Your Garden,* and contributes articles to *Gardeners' World Magazine* and *Garden Answers*. He has lectured and travelled extensively all over the world and seen many houseplants growing in their natural habitats. His own houseplant collection is increasing rapidly.

CONTENTS

INTRODUCTION

If you are one of the many people who complain that 'I always kill houseplants', don't give up, this book is for you. And if you have a thriving collection already, I hope that it will encourage you to grow some more. There is an indescribable excitement as the first flower buds appear, your foliage plants flourish, or a room becomes a kaleidoscope of colour - it is certainly not to be missed. There are hundreds of houseplants to grow. Be adventurous and let the pictures in this book tempt you to go out and buy - there will certainly be many to suit your taste and needs. You must grow houseplants; they are fascinating, fun and a valuable addition to the home. Here's wishing you years of success.

Matthew Biggs

PLANTS IN A-Z SEQUENCE

Achimenes
'Johanna Michelssen'
Hot water plant • Page 22

Aeschynanthus
'Mona Lisa'
Lipstick vine • Page 24

Aglaonema
'Maria'
Chinese evergreen • Page 26

Asparagus densiflorus
'Sprengeri'
Asparagus fern • Page 32

Asparagus
falcatus
Asparagus fern • Page 32

Asparagus
setaceus
Asparagus fern • Page 32

Aspidistra
elatior
Cast-iron plant • Page 34

Begonia
masoniana
Begonia • Page 38

Begonia rex
hybrids
Begonia • Page 38

Calathea
makoyana
Peacock plant • Pages 40-43

Aglaonema
'Lillian'
Chinese evergreen • Page 26

Anthurium andreanum
'Carré'
Flamingo flower • Page 28

Anthurium
scherzerianum
Flamingo flower • Page 28

Aphelandra squarrosa
'Louisae'
Zebra plant • Page 30

Begonia
maculata
Begonia • Page 36

Pendulous
begonia
Begonia • Page 36

Begonia
'Elatior' hybrid
Begonia • Page 36

Begonia boweri
'Tiger Paws'
Begonia • Page 38

Calathea
zebrina
Peacock plant • Pages 40-43

Ctenanthe 'Golden Mosaic'
(related to *Calathea)*
Peacock plant • Pages 40-43

Stromanthe 'Stripestar'
(related to *Calathea)*
Peacock plant • Pages 40-43

Chlorophytum comosum
'Variegatum'
Spider plant • Page 44

Cissus rhombifolia
Grape ivy • Page 46

Cissus rhombifolia 'Ellen Danica'
Grape ivy • Page 46

Clivia miniata
Kaffir lily • Page 48

Cordyline fruticosa 'Kiwi'
Ti plant • Page 54

Cordyline fruticosa 'Lord Robertson'
Ti plant • Page 54

Dieffenbachia 'Camilla'
Dumb cane • Page 60

Dieffenbachia seguine 'Tropic Snow'
Dumb cane • Page 60

Dieffenbachia 'Veerle Compacta'
Dumb cane • Page 60

Dracaena deremensis 'Green Stripe'
Dracaena • Page 62

Codiaeum
'Red Curl'
Croton • Page 50

Codiaeum
'Goldstar'
Croton • Page 50

Codiaeum
'Petra'
Croton • Page 50

Columnea
'Wilde Brand'
Goldfish plant • Page 52

Cordyline fruticosa
'Red Edge'
Ti plant • Page 54

Cyclamen
cultivar
Cyclamen • Page 56

Cyperus
albostriatus
Umbrella plant • Page 58

Cyperus
cyperoides
Umbrella plant • Page 58

Dracaena fragrans
'Massangeana'
Dracaena • Page 62

Epipremnum
aureum
Devil's ivy • Page 64

Epipremnum
'Marble Queen'
Devil's ivy • Page 64

Epipremnum 'Neon'
Devil's ivy • Page 64

Euphorbia pulcherrima
Poinsettia • Page 66

Fatsia japonica
Japanese aralia • Page 68

Ficus elastica 'Robusta'
Rubber plant • Page 72

Ficus lyrata 'Audrey' featured with
Rubber plant • Page 72

Hedera canariensis 'Montgomery'
Ivy • Page 78

Hedera helix 'Goldchild'
Ivy • Page 78

x Fatshedera lizei 'Pia'
featured with
Japanese aralia • Page 68

Ficus benjamina
'De Gantel'
Weeping fig • Page 70

Ficus benjamina
(with plaited stems)
Weeping fig • Page 70

Ficus elastica
'Tineke'
Rubber plant • Page 72

Fittonia verschaffeltii var.
argyroneura 'Nana'
Mosaic plant • Page 74

Fittonia v. var. *pearcei*
'Superba Red'
Mosaic plant • Page 74

Gardenia
augusta
Cape jessamine • Page 76

Hedera algeriensis
'Gloire de Marengo'
Ivy • Page 78

Hedera helix
'Mini Heron'
Ivy • Page 78

Hedera helix
'Pittsburgh'
Ivy • Page 78

Hibiscus rosa-sinensis
'Paramaribo'
Rose of China • Page 80

Hoya carnosa
'Tricolor'
Wax plant • Page 82

Hoya lanceolata
spp. *bella*
Wax plant • Page 82

Hydrangea macrophylla
'Libelle'
Mophead hydrangea • Page 84

Hydrangea macrophylla
'Bodensee'
Mophead hydrangea • Page 84

Jasminum
officinale
Jasmine • Page 90

Justicia
brandegeeana
Shrimp plant • Page 92

Kalanchoe
blossfeldiana
Flaming Katy • Page 94

Kalanchoe pumila
featured with
Flaming Katy • Page 94

Maranta leuconeura
var. *erythroneura*
Rabbit's foot plant • Page 96

Maranta leuconeura
var. *kerchoveana*
Rabbit's foot plant • Page 96

Monstera
deliciosa
Swiss cheese plant • Page 98

Nolina
recurvata
Pony tail palm • Page 100

Hypoestes phyllostachya
Polkadot plant • Page 86

Impatiens
Busy Lizzie • Page 88

Kalanchoe 'Tessa' featured with
Flaming Katy • Page 94

Large-flowered and 'mini-zonal' *Pelargonium*
Geranium • Page 102

Pelargonium graveolens
Geranium • Page 102

Peperomia caperata 'Luna'
Pepper elder • Page 104

Peperomia obtusifolia
'Green Gold'
Pepper elder • Page 104

Philodendron erubescens
'Imperial Red'
Sweetheart plant • Page 106

Philodendron
'Medisa'
Sweetheart plant • Page 106

Philodendron scandens
Sweetheart plant • Page 106

Radermachera sinica
Emerald tree • Page 112

Rhododendron
'Rosali'
Azalea • Page 114

Rhododendron
(standard form)
Azalea • Page 122

Saintpaulia
'Ramona'
African violet • Page 116

Schefflera
'Amate'
Umbrella tree • Page 122

Schefflera arboricola
'Compacta'
Umbrella tree • Page 122

Schefflera arboricola
'Trinette'
Umbrella tree • Page 122

Sinningia
cultivar
Gloxinia • Page 124

Pilea
'Moon Valley'
Aluminium plant • Page 108

Pilea
cadieri
Aluminium plant • Page 108

Plectranthus coleoides
'Marginatus'
Candle plant • Page 110

Sansevieria trifasciata
Mother-in-law's tongue • Page 118

S. t. 'Laurentii'

S. t. 'Golden Futura'

S. t. 'Golden Hahnii'

Saxifraga
stolonifera
Mother of thousands • Page 120

Saxifraga stolonifera
'Tricolor'
Mother of thousands • Page 120

Solanum
pseudocapsicum
Jerusalem cherry • Page 126

Capsicum annuum
featured with
Jerusalem cherry • Page 126

Soleirolia soleirolii
'Aurea'
Baby's tears • Page 128

Solenostemon
varieties
Coleus • Page 130

Spathiphyllum
'Cupido'
Peace lily • Page 132

Stephanotis
floribunda
Madagascar jasmine • Page 134

Streptocarpus
'Maassen's White'
Cape primrose • Page 136

Syngonium
'Arrow'
Goosefoot plant • Page 138

Tolmiea menziesii
'Taff's Gold'
Piggyback plant • Page 140

Tradescantia
varieties
Spiderwort • Page 142

Yucca
elephantipes
Yucca • Page 144

Spathiphyllum
'Sensation'
Peace lily • Page 132

Syngonium
'Infrared'
Goosefoot plant • Page 138

Yucca elephantipes
'Jewel'
Yucca • Page 144

BROMELIADS

Aechmea
fasciata
Bromeliads • Pages 146-149

Ananas
comosus
Bromeliads • Pages 146-149

Cryptanthus
bivittatus
Bromeliads • Pages 146-149

Guzmania
'Rana'
Bromeliads • Pages 146-149

Neoregelia
'Tricolor Perfecta'
Bromeliads • Pages 146-149

Tillandsia
(air plant)
Bromeliads • Pages 146-149

Vriesea
'Fire'
Bromeliads • Pages 146-149

INDOOR BULBS

Hippeastrum
'Minerva'
Indoor bulbs • Page 150

Hyacinth
'Blue Delft'
Indoor bulbs • Page 150

DESERT CACTI

Cleistocactus strausii
Desert cacti • Page 152

Parodia scopa
Desert cacti • Page 152

Echinopsis chamaecereus
Desert cacti • Page 152

Mammillaria baumii
Desert cacti • Page 152

FOREST CACTI

Epiphyllum
'Pegasus'
Forest cacti • Page 154

Schlumbergera
hybrid
Forest cacti • Page 154

FERNS

Adiantum bicolor
Ferns • Pages 156-159

Adiantum capillus-veneris
Ferns • Pages 156-159

Asplenium nidus
Ferns • Pages 156-159

Blechnum gibbum
Ferns Pages 156-159

Cyrtomium falcatum
Ferns • Pages 156-159

Didymochlaena truncatula
Ferns • Pages 156-159

Dryopteris erythrosora
Ferns • Pages 156-159

Nephrolepis exaltata 'Dallas Jewel'
Ferns • Pages 156-159

Pellaea rotundifolia
Ferns • Pages 156-159

Platycerium bifurcatur
Ferns • Pages 156-159

Pteris cretica 'Albolineata'
Ferns • Pages 156-159

PALMS

Caryota mitis
Palms • Pages 156-159

Chamaedora elegans
Palms • Pages 156-159

Chrysalidocarpus lutescens
Palms • Pages 156-159

Howea forsteriana
Palms • Pages 156-159

Phoenix canariensis
Palms • Pages 156-159

SUCCULENTS

Crassula ovata
Succulents • Page 164

Haworthia attenuata
Succulents • Page 164

Echeveria 'Perle von Nurnberg'
Succulents • Page 164

Echeveria 'Black Prince'
Succulents • Page 164

x *Pachyveria* hybrid
Succulents • Page 164

TEMPORARY DISPLAYS

Browallia speciosa
Temporary displays
Pages 166-169

Catharanthus roseus
Temporary displays
Pages 166-169

Dendranthema x *grandiflorum*
Temporary displays
Pages 166-169

Eustoma grandiflorum
Temporary displays • Pages 166-169

Exacum affine
Temporary displays • Pages 166-169

Gerbera jamesonii
Temporary displays • Pages 166-169

Senecio cruentus
Temporary displays
Pages 166-169

Primula obconica
Temporary displays • Pages 166-169

ACHIMENES

From early summer until autumn, this delightful little plant produces masses of short-lived flowers in constant succession. There are hundreds of brightly coloured cultivars available, in shades of red and white to pink and apricot. Many have thin trailing stems, which makes them ideal for hanging baskets, but they are just as effective when carefully pruned and supported by thin canes.

Achimenes need bright light away from summer sun, moderate to warm conditions and humidity provided by occasional misting with tepid water, by standing the pot on a tray of moist gravel filled with water to just below the base of the pot or by grouping several plants together. They have dormant and active stages in their annual growth, which begins in late winter to mid-spring, as soon as temperatures rise and remain constant. When the first shoots appear, water just a little at first, gradually increasing the amount as more growth develops. Although the majority of achimenes are naturally trailing plants, you can encourage bushy growth by pinching back the young stems. In early autumn, when fewer flowers appear and the leaves lose their vigour, stop feeding and gradually reduce watering until the leaves die back and the plant finally becomes dormant. At this stage, stop watering altogether, remove the dead leaves, label the pot and store it in a cool, dry, frost-free place over winter. In spring, replant the largest tubers in fresh compost and begin the cycle again.

PROPAGATION

Plant *Achimenes* tubers in John Innes No. 2 or in a 50-50 mix of peat substitute-based compost and sharp sand or perlite. Space them 1.25cm apart and 2cm deep in a 7.5-10cm pot. Moisten the soil with soft, tepid water and place the pot in an airing cupboard or propagator to stimulate growth. Check the pot daily and when shoots appear, move it into a bright, warm room Alternatively, start the tubers into growth on a warm windowsill in mid- to late spring.

FEEDING AND WATERING

When in full growth, use tepid water to keep the soil constantly moist. Feed every two weeks throughout the summer with flowering houseplant fertilizer.

PESTS AND PROBLEMS

Splashing water on the leaves or over-wetting when misting may cause scorching. In excessively high temperatures the flower buds become brown. Pests are rarely a problem, but look out for aphids. Squash these by hand or spray them carefully with a soft soap solution.

LONGEVITY

Selecting the best tubers each year means that the original plant can provide material for many years.

Right: *The small rhizomes or underground stems of achimenes are covered with scales that look like small pine cones. In the past it was widely, yet wrongly, believed that they could only be encouraged into growth and watered with hot water. Hence their common name of 'hot water plant'.*

Right: There is an extraordinary range of colours, shades and flower markings available among achimenes. This beautiful purple-flowered cultivar is one called 'Martha Peschel'.

Right: Achimenes *'Prima Donna' is a bushy, self-supporting cultivar that is very free-flowering over a long period. The brightly coloured scarlet blooms have yellow and brown spotted centres. This is a cheerful, good value plant.*

Right: This is 'Johanna Michelssen', a neat, self-supporting plant with vivid, almost glowing pink flowers and striped centres. It is the perfect colour for a high-profile display.

AESCHYNANTHUS

Where better to find the tropical touch than the rainforests of Southeast Asia, home of the exotic *Aeschynanthus?* Its long trailing stems, clothed in fleshy leaves, are crowned in summer with clusters of exquisite flowers and buds like coloured lipsticks. A hanging basket shows them off to their best advantage. They are ideal for the conservatory, yet with care can also be grown successfully in the home.

Despite its exotic origins, *Aeschynanthus* is surprisingly tolerant of conditions in the home. Avoid direct sunshine, but bright light, particularly during the winter, is vital to promote flowering the following year. Plants need constant warmth and dislike fluctuations, although they can tolerate cooler conditions for a few days if the compost is kept slightly dry. Stand the pot on a tray of moistened gravel and remember to top up the water level regularly. If your plant is in a hanging basket, put the tray just below the trailing stems. High humidity is particularly important at higher temperatures. With *Aeschynanthus,* it is safer to avoid the common practice of misting plants to increase humidity as the leaves scorch easily, unless, of course, you use a fine spray and are prepared to take a risk. After two to three years, when the pot is full of roots, lift the plant out, carefully tease away the old compost from the roots and replant it in a pot one size larger, using new potting mixture. Alternatively, when the older stems become bare, lift the plant, trim the roots to two-thirds their original length, replace the compost and replant in the same pot. An open peat-substitute houseplant potting mixture is ideal for these plants.

PROPAGATION

Take tip cuttings from healthy, non-flowering shoots in spring or summer.

1 *Trim the cutting just below the leaf joint.*
2 *Remove the lower leaves.*
3 *Plant three or four cuttings in a shallow 13cm pot.*
4 *Place the pot in a plastic bag supported with canes. Once the cuttings have rooted - after four weeks or so - and are growing, repot them into individual containers. Stand them in a warm position on pebbles in a water-filled tray to maintain high humidity.*

FEEDING AND WATERING

When the plant is growing, water it regularly to keep the compost moist. Allow the surface to dry out slightly between waterings and reduce watering in winter. Feed every fortnight in summer and monthly during winter with a flowering houseplant fertilizer.

PESTS AND PROBLEMS

Aeschynanthus are usually trouble-free, but check plants regularly, as aphids may be a problem and small infestations are easier to deal with. Water on the leaves causes scorching and unsightly brown spots. Exposure to cold draughts causes the leaves to drop.

LONGEVITY

If pruned back to the edge of the container every two to three years after flowering and fed well in summer, lipstick vines can last for many years.

POINT TO NOTE

Aeschynanthus radicans is now the correct botanical name for *A. lobbianus,* the lipstick vine. You may also see it labelled in garden centres and nurseries as *A. longiflorus* or *A. javanicus.*

Below: *The bright crimson flowers of* Aeschynanthus *'Purple Star' are found towards the end of the stems, emerging from the base of the leaves. Their colour shows up well against a pale wall.*

Right: *The dark green leaves of* Aeschynanthus *'Mona Lisa' are a perfect foil for its superb display of bright red flowers.*

Left: *Some varieties, such as this stunning* Aeschynanthus *'Carina' have a more upright habit, at least initially.*

Right: *In close up, it is easy to understand the common name for these plants, as the vivid flowers emerge from the dark calyces like lipsticks from their cases.*

AGLAONEMA

Beautiful leaves patterned in pale shades are the chief attraction of this handsome, slow-growing foliage plant, whose original home is on the forest floors of Southeast Asia. Mature plants occasionally produce white sail-like flowers. Also with age, the plant sheds its lower leaves, leaving attractive bronze rings around the dark green stems.

1

Aglaonemas are happiest in moderate light. They will tolerate low light levels but not permanently, so if they are growing in a shady position, bring them into brighter light regularly to boost growth. They enjoy moderate temperatures, but dislike fluctuations, draughts or excessive warmth, although they will tolerate lower temperatures when watering is reduced. Given their native habitat, it is not surprising that aglaonemas need constant humidity, so either mist them regularly with tepid water, group plants together or stand them on a shallow tray of pebbles filled with water to just below the base of the pot.

Repot aglaonemas every two to three years in mid-spring into a shallow pot one size larger than the previous one and water with tepid water. Use John Innes No. 2 with added horticultural grit or a peat substitute-based compost. Once plants have reached maturity, topdress them annually by carefully removing and replacing the top 5cm of compost, and when they have reached the maximum pot size, replace the old compost completely every three years.

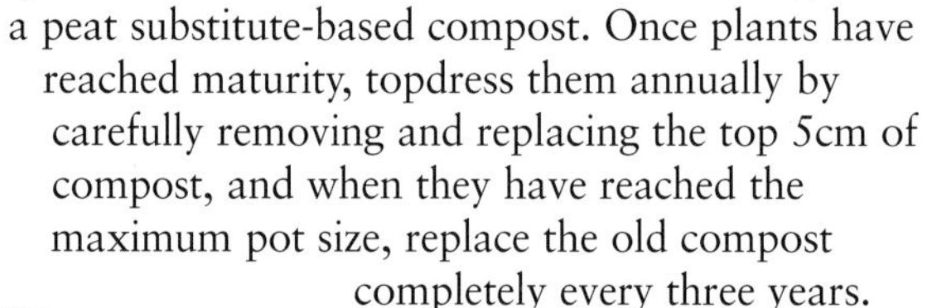

2

3

PROPAGATION
Shoot tip cuttings 10cm long will root in moist cutting compost, or you can divide plants in mid- to late spring.

1 *Carefully divide the plant, taking basal shoots or suckers with several leaves attached.*
2 *Pot each division into a pot of growing compost, here a peat substitute mixture.*
3 *Place four canes in each pot, cover the pot with a plastic bag and place it in a warm place in bright light. Rooting takes six to eight weeks. Pot on young plants annually.*

FEEDING AND WATERING
When the plant is actively growing, keep the compost moist using tepid water and allow the surface to dry out between waterings. Feed with a liquid fertilizer for foliage houseplants every two weeks. If the plant is in a cool room in winter, water it sparingly, keeping the compost just moist and feed it monthly.

PESTS AND PROBLEMS
Aglaonemas are usually trouble-free, but can suffer from mealy bug and red spider mite in dry conditions.

Browning of the leaf tips and margins is caused by dry air, so increase humidity. In low temperatures or draughty conditions, leaves may curl up and margins become brown; move the plant to a warmer, draught-free position.

In cool conditions or if overwatered, the leaves turn yellow. Allow the compost to dry out, then water carefully, keeping the compost moderately moist or move the plant to a warmer position.

LONGEVITY
Aglaonemas take several years to reach their full glory and with care are long-lived.

Left: The elegant leaves of Aglaonema 'Maria' are dark green and marbled with silver-grey and green patches. Like all the aglaonemas, the subtle leaf markings make them ideal for rooms decorated with subdued colours.

Above: *Aglaonema 'Silver Queen' is a popular variety with narrow leaves and silvery white markings.*

A close look at one of the leaves of Aglaonema 'Lillian' reveals their true beauty. If you admire them from a distance or at close quarters, they are magnificent plants.

Above: *Aglaonema 'Lillian', a graceful plant with grey bands along the lateral veins. Compact in growth, it is ideal for grouping with other plants.*

FLAMINGO FLOWER

ANTHURIUM

The glossy leaves are an attractive feature and when its blooms appear, *Anthurium* makes an instant impact. It is impossible to ignore the vibrantly coloured spathes that appear like plastic shields among the foliage and the tail-like projections carrying the clusters of true flowers. Given adequate warmth and humidity, this wonderful houseplant will flower almost continuously.

Coming from the rainforest and grown as garden plants in the tropics, it is no surprise that warmth, moist compost and humidity are needed to grow these beauties. Constant warmth is vital to encourage growth and flower production; in low temperatures plants become dormant, and in fluctuating temperatures or draughts they may produce deformed leaves and existing leaves may turn yellow. If the room temperature is comfortable for you, then *Anthurium* should be happy, too. It also needs bright light throughout the year away from direct sunshine, which causes scorching or misshapen leaves. Frequent misting with tepid water or standing the pot on a tray of moist pebbles keeps humidity high, but *A. scherzerianum* is more tolerant of lower humidity than its relatives. To see the glossy leaves at their best, remove any dust by softly sponging them with warm water. Repot annually in spring when the compost becomes congested with roots into a pot one size larger using a potting mix of three parts peat-substitute compost with one part added sphagnum moss.

1

PROPAGATION

Divide plants every two or three years when they are repotted in spring.

1 *Carefully lift the plant from its pot and gently tease away excess compost from the roots. Separate the divisions.*

2 *Repot each division into new compost in a 10 or 13cm pot, ensuring that the growing point is above the compost. Keep the surrounding air constantly humid until the new plants establish. The ideal potting mixture is the same as that described for repotting the parent plant. Water the repotted divisions thoroughly and stand them in a warm, bright position.*

FEEDING AND WATERING

The compost should be kept moist but not waterlogged, using tepid water. If this happens by mistake, allow it to dry out, checking daily, and begin watering again when the compost surface dries out. In winter, reduce watering, keeping the compost just moist. This is particularly important in cooler conditions. Feed with a flowering houseplant fertilizer every two weeks in summer and monthly in winter.

PESTS AND PROBLEMS

If the surrounding air is too dry, leaf tips will turn brown and red spider mite may appear. Look for fine webbing around the leaves and stem, punctuated by tiny yellow dots. Control the mites by spraying them with organic houseplant insecticide and increasing air humidity by regular misting with tepid water. Check houseplants for pests every day.

LONGEVITY

Over the years, you can take many divisions from the parent, so one plant will give you a regular supply of plants to replace older specimens.

Left: *With their curly spadices and bright red, waxy spathes,* A. scherzerianum *has remarkable flower heads, even for an anthurium!*

Below: *If you want to bring a touch of the tropics into your home,* Anthurium andreanum *'Carré', with its eye-catching orange-red flower heads, is certainly worth considering.*

Below: *The dark leaves of* A. andreanum *'Acropolis' provide an ideal background for the glossy, snow-white spathes.*

APHELANDRA

This regal evergreen is worth growing for its foliage alone. The dark green leaves with ivory veining are highly ornamental and there is the added attraction of brightly coloured flowering spikes that last for many months. This native of the Brazilian rainforest appreciates warmth and humidity and although often discarded after flowering, it can be kept for several years.

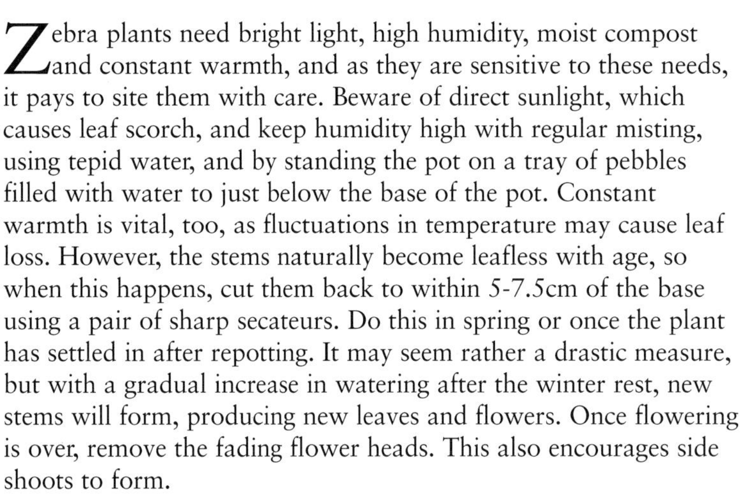

Zebra plants need bright light, high humidity, moist compost and constant warmth, and as they are sensitive to these needs, it pays to site them with care. Beware of direct sunlight, which causes leaf scorch, and keep humidity high with regular misting, using tepid water, and by standing the pot on a tray of pebbles filled with water to just below the base of the pot. Constant warmth is vital, too, as fluctuations in temperature may cause leaf loss. However, the stems naturally become leafless with age, so when this happens, cut them back to within 5-7.5cm of the base using a pair of sharp secateurs. Do this in spring or once the plant has settled in after repotting. It may seem rather a drastic measure, but with a gradual increase in watering after the winter rest, new stems will form, producing new leaves and flowers. Once flowering is over, remove the fading flower heads. This also encourages side shoots to form.

Before growth starts in late winter or early spring, remove the plant from its pot, gently tease the old potting mixture from the roots and repot it into a peat substitute-based mixture, using a pot one size larger. Do this when the compost becomes congested with roots. Water plants thoroughly after repotting them.

PROPAGATION

The material removed by pruning in spring or healthy 5-7.5cm-long side shoots are ideal for cuttings.

1 *Trim just below a leaf joint with a sharp knife and remove the bottom leaves.*

2 *Fill a pot with cutting mixture, firm it and make several shallow holes with a dibber. Dip the cuttings in hormone rooting powder, tap off the excess and insert them to just below the basal leaves. Put several cuttings in each pot, stand four canes in the pot and water the compost.*

3 *Place the pot in a plastic bag, secure the top and put it in a bright spot. When the cuttings root and growth starts, take them from the bag and leave them for about a week to acclimatize before potting each one separately.*

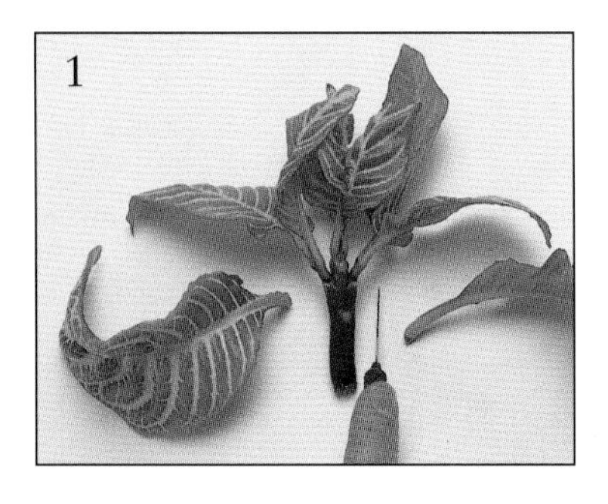
1

2

3

FEEDING AND WATERING

Keep the compost moist with soft tepid water, but do not overwater. In winter, the plant can withstand lower temperatures if you reduce watering, but do not allow the roots to dry out. From spring to summer, when the plant is growing, feed it every week with a general fertilizer.

PESTS AND PROBLEMS

The most common problem - loss of leaves - can be caused by several factors: draughts, low temperatures, direct sunshine, dryness at the roots and dry air, which can also cause browning of the leaf tips and margins. Look for telltale signs and remedy the problem immediately.

If the surrounding atmosphere is too dry, red spider mite can be a problem. Look out for mottling of the leaves and in severe cases, fine webbing around the growth tips and leaves, dotted with translucent orange mites.

Scale insect and mealy bug can also cause problems.

LONGEVITY

With care, zebra plants can last for a few years before they need replacing.

Below: Aphelandra squarrosa *'Dania' is a compact plant with glossy leaves, crowned with clusters of bright yellow bracts.*

Right: *The large bold leaves of* Aphelandra squarrosa *'Brockfield' are an impressive sight. Wipe them with a soft, damp cloth to remove dust.*

Above: Aphelandra squarrosa *'Louisae' has highly decorative yellow bracts tipped with burnt orange markings. Yellow flowers appear from the bracts.*

ASPARAGUS

If you are about to buy your first houseplants and are looking for something to give you encouragement, why not try the ornamental asparagus? Although known as 'ferns', these wonderful foliage plants are part of the lily family and are much easier to grow. Tough, tolerant and undemanding, yet graceful in appearance, they are ideal plants to inspire confidence in beginners.

One of the attributes of ornamental asparagus is their ability to withstand low and fluctuating temperatures, drought, occasional overwatering and regular neglect. However, with a little care, it is very easy to produce healthy, flourishing plants. Provide moderate temperatures all year, away from the effects of radiators or the summer sun at midday. The plants tolerate higher or lower temperatures, providing these remain above freezing. Bright light, away from direct sunlight is ideal, but the plant will grow in partial shade and is a valuable asset in dull corners, although growth is slow. High humidity is not essential, but occasional misting helps, particularly in heated rooms. Repot asparagus annually in spring or when the compost is congested with roots, using John Innes No. 2. Yellowing foliage with brown margins or even leaf drop is usually caused by too much sunshine or dryness at the roots for a prolonged period. Yellow foliage may also result if temperatures are too high or if there is insufficient light. Remove any affected stems and move the plant to a more suitable position.

1

PROPAGATION
Divide large specimens in spring. Even the smallest sections of this vigorous plant can make new subjects.

1 *Lift the plant from the pot and shake the excess compost from the tuberous roots. Divide the plant into 7.5-10cm sections. As the plant is very tough, you will probably need to use an old kitchen knife or even a saw.*
2 *Start off the pieces in 15cm pots and plant them so that the tops are about 2.5cm above the surface. Place in a bright spot and water well.*

2

FEEDING AND WATERING
Water thoroughly in the growing season, but avoid waterlogging. Water less in winter. If you are inclined to forget to water your plants, asparagus ferns will survive drought for several weeks, but try to remember them more often; their tolerance is better regarded as a safety precaution than as an excuse for neglect. A weekly feed in summer and monthly in winter using foliage house-plant fertilizer keeps plants healthy and vigorous.

PESTS AND PROBLEMS
Red spider mite can be a problem, particularly when the air is dry. Look out for fine webbing and mottling of the leaves. Spray the plants with organic houseplant insecticide and with tepid water to increase humidity.

LONGEVITY
Because of their robust nature, ornamental asparagus are likely to last for many years.

OTHER CULTIVARS OF INTEREST
A densiflorus 'Myers' (foxtail fern): Huge plumes of leaves are projected on stiff stems, like giant bottlebrushes that can grow up to 90cm long. Display it in a pot.
A. plumosus 'Nanus': A compact climber that will grow up trellis or canes. Florists use it for carnation buttonholes.
A. umbellatus: Upright in growth and thornless, this pretty asparagus is a native of the Canary Islands.

Above: *The delicate feathery fronds of* A. setaceus (A. plumosus) *is made up of tiny flattened stems, not true leaves.*

Left: A. densiflorus 'Sprengeri'. *Arching stems and billowing foliage give this asparagus a graceful habit. Display it on a plinth or in a hanging basket to see it at its best.*

Right: A. falcatus *(sicklethorn). This climbing, woody-stemmed asparagus has flat, sickle-shaped leaves, bell-like flowers and sharp thorns.*

Cast-iron plant

Aspidistra

The aspidistra's resilience is legendary and any plant that can withstand low light, drought, draughts and neglect is certain to be welcomed into the home. Its dark green leaves have a stately presence and over many years the plant fills even the largest pot. Look out for flowers appearing just above the surface of the compost; in their native habitat these are pollinated by slugs!

Aspidistras need moderate temperatures and light levels to flourish. Although their tolerance of other conditions is considerable, do not presume upon their good nature; a well-tended, healthy plant is more attractive than a neglected specimen languishing in a dark corner. In poor light, aspidistras tend to remain inactive and in direct sunshine they soon suffer from leaf scorch.

Aspidistras prefer warmth; although they will grow in cooler conditions, they are not frost-hardy. They are perfectly contented in the unheated home, but dry, centrally heated air eventually creates problems, such as browning of the leaf tips and the unwelcome appearance of red spider mite. High temperatures over a long period are stressful, but the plants can survive them for short periods.

Moderate humidity is best, so mist the plants occasionally. Washing the leaves with a damp sponge to remove household dust also increases humidity. Aspidistras dislike regular root disturbance, so repot them every four years or so in spring, into a container one size larger, using John Innes No. 2 and water thoroughly.

Propagation

Divide potbound plants in spring at the same time as repotting them. Lift and then divide the rhizome by cutting off the outer parts. To retain a large clump, remove the outer sections and repot, otherwise divide the whole plant.

1 Each small section should have one pair of leaves.
2 Plant the pieces just below the surface in a 10-13cm pot using John Innes No 2 compost. Water thoroughly.
3 Treat divisions as mature specimens but do not feed for the first year.

1

2

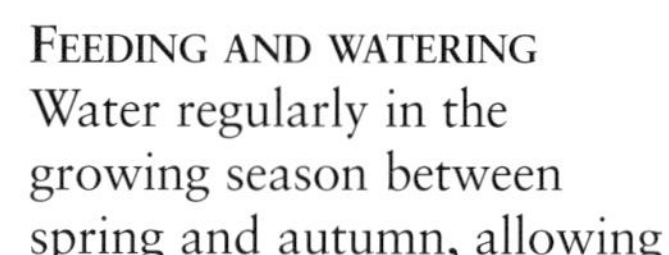

3

Feeding and watering

Water regularly in the growing season between spring and autumn, allowing the top of the compost to dry out between waterings. Reduce watering in the winter. In spring, gradually increase feeding and watering as new growth appears. Beware of overwatering; it may result in leaf spot or rotting of the underground stems and is a sure way to kill an aspidistra.

Pests and problems

In a hot, dry atmosphere, red spider mites are likely to be a problem. Look for mottling and bronzing on the leaves; in the later stages, fine webbing appears. Spray with organic insecticide and increase humidity by regularly spraying with tepid water.

Dry air also causes the leaf tips to turn brown.

Longevity

Aspidistras are renowned for their longevity and can survive for many years.

Below: *The leaves of* Aspidistra elatior *'Variegata' are boldly and irregularly striped. To grow well and keep its variegation, it needs more light than the green-leaved varieties. Too much fertilizer can also cause loss of variegation.*

OTHER CULTIVARS OF INTEREST
A. elatior 'Milky Way': Small creamy spots covering the leaves.
A. lurida 'Irish Mist': The green leaves are speckled with yellow.

Left: Aspidistra elatior, *with its stiff, upright stems and broad, strap-shaped leaves, was much-loved as a houseplant in Victorian England. It withstands variable growing conditions, but dislikes constant repotting or waterlogged compost.*

BEGONIA

Usually flowering during late summer, tuberous-rooted begonias are renowned for their large, delicate yet brightly coloured flowers, which are among the most spectacular of any pot plant. Cane-stemmed begonias are easy-to-grow and make good all-round plants for any collection, while the semperflorens begonias, popular as summer bedding plants, are equally at home as houseplants.

Tuberous rooted begonias need good, bright light and are better grown in a greenhouse and brought indoors into a bright warm position to flower. In spring, plant the tuber, hollow side up, in a pot of peat substitute-based compost, lightly covering the top. Place it in a warm bright position. Water sparingly when the first shoots emerge and increase the amount as more growth appears. Keep the compost moist throughout the growing season and maintain humidity by standing plants on a tray of moist pebbles and lightly misting plants that are not flowering. In the autumn, reduce watering as the foliage dies down and stop when it turns completely yellow. Remove the foliage when it has completely died back, then label and store the dry tubers over winter in a cool room. Tubers have a variable lifespan and should be repropagated when they lose their vigour.

Cane stemmed begonias are vigorous plants with jointed stems like green bamboos and many are grown for their spotted 'angels wing' leaves, which in some varieties are lobed or split. The long-lasting, hanging clusters of flowers in shades of pink and orange to white appear from early summer to winter. They need constant bright light. Plants that have outgrown their allotted space can be cut back to a leaf joint near the base in spring. After they have produced new stems, cut these back to two or three leaf joints to encourage bushy growth.

Semperflorens begonias produce a vibrant floral display throughout the year. Glossy foliage adds to their attraction and those with bronze or variegated leaves are particularly striking. They are excellent, easy plants for a cool room and need bright light away from direct sunlight. Pinch out the growth tips of young plants to encourage bushiness and grow in half pots or pans. They flower better when deadheaded regularly and if they are slightly potbound.

1

2

PROPAGATION

Propagate tuberous-rooted begonias from tip cuttings.

1 *Cut off a non-flowering shoot about 10cm long, trim below a leaf joint and remove the lower leaves.*

2 *Dip the base of the cutting in hormone rooting powder, gently tap off the excess and insert into a pot of moist cutting compost.*

Propagate cane-stemmed begonias using tip cuttings as explained above. Cuttings will also root in water and should be potted into a peat substitute compost.

In semperflorens begonias, the single-flowered types can be grown from spring sown seed or cuttings; other varieties from tip cuttings.

FEEDING AND WATERING

Water tuberous begonias sparingly in spring as the first shoots emerge and increase the amount as more appear. Reduce watering in autumn as the leaves die back. Feed every two weeks with a general houseplant fertilizer when the plant is growing. Others, keep moist in the growing season; reduce watering in winter.

PESTS AND PROBLEMS

Aphids and red spider mite can be a problem.

Grey mould forms on the leaves when cold and damp. Improve the ventilation.

The leaves become yellow when the plant is in low light, overwatered, underwatered and in low temperatures. If humidity is too low, the leaf tips become brown. Stand the pot on a tray of pebbles filled with water to just below the base of the pot.

The flower buds fall if a plant is underwatered or in dry air. Increase watering and humidity.

LONGEVITY

Some varieties will last for a few years; others can be kept for many years.

Left: *Pendulous types of begonia have trailing stems and are best grown in a hanging basket or in a pot on a plinth. The colourful blooms are produced towards the ends of the stems.*

Left: *There are many flower colours to choose among the compact 'Elatior' or 'Reiger' begonias and their vivid shades contrast perfectly with the dark green, glossy leaves. Treat these as temporary displays or keep them going for several years.*

Left: *Removing the leaves from a cane-stemmed begonia creates a 'tree-like' result. Many of the taller varieties need staking, but all are excellent plants for foliage and flowers. This striking one is* Begonia maculata.

BEGONIA REX

'King of begonias' - what an appropriate name for a wonderful plant and the parent of a collection of cultivars whose textured leaves in the myriad colours of a painter's palette are among the most stunningly beautiful of any houseplant. If that doesn't encourage you to grow them, these begonias also tolerate occasional drought and some neglect, making them a highly attractive proposition for any collector.

The ideal position for begonias is in good, bright light away from direct sunshine, although they will tolerate light shade. Conditions should be moderate to warm, but like many houseplants, begonias tolerate slightly lower temperatures if you water them carefully. It is vital that you keep plants away from draughts and from the dry air that usually accompanies high temperatures. To maintain humidity, stand plants on a tray of pebbles filled with water to just below the base of the pot. Avoid misting them, however, as this can cause the stems to rot.

Healthy plants grow quickly; repot them every spring into a half pot or pan of John Innes No 2 or peat-substitute compost with added sharp sand or perlite to help drainage. Water them well.

PROPAGATION
Propagate large-leaved begonias from leaf cuttings.

1 *Take a healthy leaf and place it upside-down on a firm surface. Cut off the stem close to the leaf. Make cuts about 2cm long and 2.5cm apart across the main veins.*
2 *Place the leaf the right way up on a tray of moist cutting compost. Use pebbles as weights or wire staples to keep the veins in contact with the compost.*
3 *Cover the tray with a transparent lid or put it in a clear plastic bag, loosely knotted at the end. Stand the tray in a warm, bright position.*
4 *After a three or four weeks small plantlets form and can be carefully repotted.*

1

2

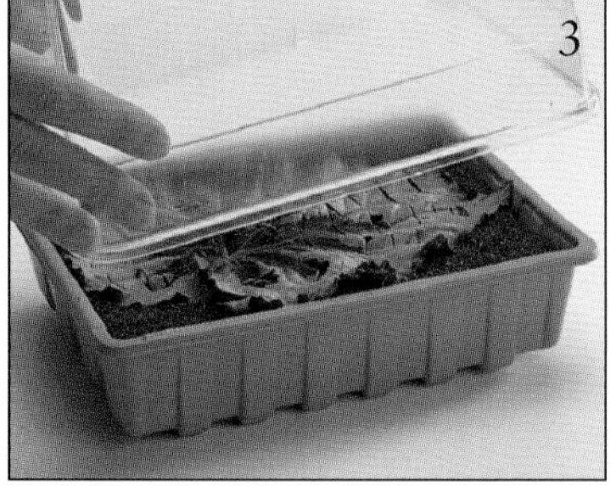
3

4

FEEDING AND WATERING
Use tepid water and allow the compost surface to dry out between waterings. Reduce watering in winter, keeping the compost slightly moist. Avoid waterlogging; use a long-spouted watering can or stand the pot in water for about an hour and then allow it to drain. Feed plants every two weeks in the growing season with a liquid feed for foliage houseplants, but stop feeding in winter.

PESTS AND PROBLEMS
Red spider mite can attack begonias. Powdery mildew can develop over leaves and shoots, which turn yellow and drop. Treat with a fungicide or remove affected parts. Do not allow the roots to remain dry for too long. Yellowing leaves may result from over-watering, draughts or low light, while brown patches on the leaves are the first signs of grey mould caused by low temperatures and cool air. Brown, papery leaf margins are caused by dry air or direct sunshine; increase humidity or move the plant.

LONGEVITY
They can live for many years.

OTHER VARIETIES OF INTEREST
Rhizomatous begonias, grown principally for their brightly coloured foliage, are related to *Begonia rex*, and include *Begonia masoniana* and *Begonia boweri* 'Tiger Paws' featured on this page. Propagate them by leaf cuttings. Other varieties include:
Begonia x 'Cleopatra',
Begonia 'Nora Bedson': A fast-growing plant with bright green leaves and chocolate-coloured spots. Easy to grow.
Begonia pustulata 'Argentea': Green leaves marked with silver streaks. Needs warm, humid conditions to flourish.

Above: *There are hundreds of different* Begonia rex *hybrids with a huge range of leaf patterns. Group several of these plants together to create a high-profile display.*

Below: Begonia boweri *'Tiger Paws' is a rhizomatous type with red blotched stems supporting shieldlike leaves with striking, bright green markings.*

Right: Begonia masoniana *is a vigorous relative of* Begonia rex, *commonly called the 'iron cross begonia' because of the dark markings on the textured leaves. They are easy plants but prone to powdery mildew.*

Peacock plant

Calathea

The leaves of these natives from the floor of the eastern Brazilian rainforest are among the most dramatic of any foliage houseplants. Pale green leaves projected on stiff, dark purple stems are patterned with bold, dark green blotches and lines, reflected in purple on their undersides. Relishing warmth and high humidity, they are ideal for a steamy, draught-free bathroom or kitchen.

For calatheas to flourish, they need almost tropical conditions. Without constant warmth and humidity, their growth slows and in cool conditions they become almost dormant and may eventually die. Provide bright, indirect light or partial shade, as direct sunshine quickly bleaches or scorches the leaves. Keep the plants in a draught-free position, with constant, moderate to high temperatures. High humidity is vital to prevent browning of the leaf margins, so mist plants regularly, using soft water to prevent calcium deposits on the leaves, group plants together or stand them on a shallow tray of moist pebbles filled with water to just below the base of the pot. Calatheas need a free-draining compost, so repot them annually in early summer in peat-substitute compost.

Stromanthe is a compact relative that needs similar growing conditions, but it is particularly susceptible to draughts and must have constant temperatures and high humidity. It is more difficult to grow. *Ctenanthe* is attractive but quite difficult to grow, it dislikes direct sunshine and low temperatures. Water it with soft tepid water and keep it in constantly warm conditions.

Propagation
Divide plants in late spring or early summer.

1 *Carefully tease the small sections apart, ensuring that each piece retains a few leaves and strong roots.*
2 *Replant in peat substitute-based compost, ensuring that the compost is firmed around the roots of the plant.*
3 *Soak each division in a bowl of soft tepid water and allow it to drain. Enclose the pot in a loosely knotted plastic bag and place it in a partially shaded position with moderate temperatures. Once new growth appears, remove the bag and leave the plant for two to three weeks to establish itself before moving it to a new position.*

Feeding and watering
Keep the compost constantly moist using soft, tepid water or rainwater. At lower temperatures, water sparingly, allowing the compost surface to dry between each watering. When the plants are actively growing, feed them every two weeks with a fertilizer for foliage houseplants. Feed every four weeks in winter.

Pests and problems
In hot, dry air or in direct sunshine, the leaf margins become brown and papery and the plant becomes susceptible to red spider mite. Move it to a bright position and increase humidity. Draughts also cause leaf curl.

Longevity
In good growing conditions, the plants last several years.

Right: Calathea *'Sanderiana' has beautiful dark leaves with fine white, pink-flushed lines. It is impossible not to be impressed by such gorgeous foliage.*

Left: The striking pattern and delicate tracery on the leaves of Calathea makoyana *has given it the accolade of being called the 'peacock plant' or 'cathedral windows'.*

Below: Sometimes, soft colours and simple leaf markings can be extremely effective, as with Ctenanthe *'Greystar'.*

Right: Ctenanthe amabilis, *sometimes labelled* Stromanthe amabilis, *is a delightful plant with glossy, silvery green, paddle-shaped leaves and dark markings. It is certainly not to be missed!*

OTHER VARIETIES OF INTEREST

Calathea concinna 'Freddy': Broad grey-green leaves with slightly undulating margins and broad, dark green markings.

Calathea lancifolia: Narrow, cigar-shaped leaves with undulating margins and dark green markings.

Below: Stromanthe *'Stripestar' has a single, pale green stripe down the midrib of each glossy outstretched leaf. The purple underside is displayed as each new leaf unfurls.*

Left: *The velvety leaves of* Calathea zebrina *have a dark green symmetrical pattern on the upper surface and purple undersides. Calatheas certainly provide you with an excellent choice, whatever your taste in houseplants.*

Right: Calathea crocata *is worth growing for the bright orange bracts that appear like exploding fireworks among the dark leaves.*

Right: Calathea *'Maui Queen' has upright growth, arching leaves and pretty markings along the midrib. Superb against a pale wall.*

Left: Ctenanthe pilosa *'Golden Mosaic' has unusual leaf patterns in a very 'modern' design. A real stunner in the right surroundings.*

CHLOROPHYTUM

This resilient houseplant, with its elegant, variegated, arching leaves, has long been a popular choice. As it matures, long wiry stems tumble over the pot and produce clusters of white flowers followed by small plantlets that give the plant the appearance of an exploding firework. Especially attractive in hanging baskets or on a stand, well-grown spider plants are a magnificent sight.

Above: *Here, roots are starting to form at the base of a plantlet.*

PROPAGATION

There are various methods of propagating spider plants. One (shown right) is to peg down the plantlets, still attached to the parent, in separate pots with a piece of bent wire. Once rooted, after six weeks or so, cut the stems from the parent.

Another way is to wait until roots begin to form, then remove and pot up the plantlets into a peat substitute-based compost or John Innes No 2.

Alternatively, remove the plantlets when roots begin to form and put them in a jar of water. When the roots are about 2.5cm long, pot them on.

Finally, you can divide the plant when repotting in spring.

Spider plants flourish in bright light and moderate warmth and appreciate regular feeding, watering and repotting. In these ideal conditions they will put on rapid growth, but they are also extremely adaptable, growing equally well in warm or cool rooms or in partial shade, although these do influence the speed of growth. Try to keep them away from draughts. In very low light, growth becomes spindly and the plants lose their variegation, while direct summer sun causes scorching. In areas where light levels are low, the plants will need some winter sunshine to keep them healthy. They will survive in a cool room if the roots are only slightly moist; indeed they prefer these conditions to the hot dry air of a centrally heated room. Here you can increase the humidity by grouping several plants together on pebbles in a tray half-filled with water or by misting the plants regularly. Mist occasionally in summer, more often if the room is warm and less so if it is cool. Check the root growth and repot plants in spring, before they become potbound, into a pot one size larger, using John Innes No. 2 or a peat-substitute compost. Fill the pots to a few centimetres below the top to allow space for watering and water thoroughly.

FEEDING AND WATERING

Whenever the plant is actively growing, keep the compost moist but not waterlogged, which soon causes rotting, and feed with a liquid general houseplant fertilizer every two weeks. At low temperatures, water sparingly, allowing the compost surface to dry out between waterings, and stop feeding.

PESTS AND PROBLEMS

Spider plants are usually pest-free, but on rare occasions aphids may be a problem.

Browning leaf tips are often a problem, usually caused by hot, dry air, particularly from central heating, or by direct sunlight. Cut off the damaged tips and move the plant to a better position. Avoid the problem by providing constant humidity and watering your plants regularly.

Pale, limp leaves caused by excessive heat and inadequate light may be a problem in winter.

LONGEVITY

Spider plants should last for many years and will provide you with masses of propagation material.

Left: Chlorophytum comosum *'Vittatum' is the variety most often seen. With care, it will rapidly grow into a fine specimen houseplant.*

Above: *Displaying spider plants in hanging pots allows the graceful leaves and trailing runners to grow unhindered.*

Above: *A comparison of leaves from three* Chlorophytum *varieties highlights the differences in their markings. From left to right:* C. comosum *'Variegatum' (green central stripe, white or cream margins); a plain green form;* C. comosum *'Vittatum' (white or cream central stripe, green margins).*

Right: Chlorophytum comosum *'Variegatum' is a handsome plant with a broad green band down the centre of each arching leaf. Robust and easy to grow.*

CISSUS

This tough, robust yet attractive vine tolerates a wide range of conditions and can grow several metres tall, clinging to its support by means of twining tendrils. Trained along trellising, the dense foliage creates a glossy green barrier that is ideal for dividing rooms; grown up a moss pole, it can develop into an impressive specimen plant. It is easy to grow and an ideal plant for cool locations.

A bright position away from direct sunshine suits *Cissus,* but it also tolerates partial and even full shade, although in lower light levels growth is slower. They are ideal plants for an unheated room or hallway, where they enjoy moderate to low temperatures and good ventilation away from the effects of central heating. It is important to increase the humidity as temperatures rise. Mist plants occasionally or stand young plants on a shallow tray of pebbles filled with water to just below the base of the pot. If the pot becomes congested with roots, repot plants into a container one size larger in spring, using John Innes No. 2 or peat substitute-based compost, and water thoroughly. Large plants which are difficult to repot should be topdressed annually by carefully removing and replacing the top 5-7.5cm of compost. Pinch out the growing tips of young plants to encourage bushy growth and when older plants become spindly and bare at the base, cut them back to between 10 and 20cm in spring, then feed and water them regularly to encourage healthy growth.

PROPAGATION

In spring or summer, take 7.5-10cm-long healthy shoot tips from the current season's side shoots to use as cuttings.

1 *Trim with a sharp knife just below a leaf joint and remove the basal leaves. Using a pencil or thin cane, make four holes a few centimetres deep in a 9cm pot of moist cutting compost. Dip the base of each cutting in hormone rooting powder, gently tapping off the excess. Insert the cuttings and firm the compost gently around the stem.*

2 *Place a plastic bag loosely over the pot, supported by a wire hoop to keep it away from the cuttings, and put it in a warm corner away from direct light. Once roots are formed and the cuttings begin to grow, remove the bag, allow the plants to acclimatize for about a week and then pot them into separate containers.*

FEEDING AND WATERING

Using tepid water, keep the compost moist but not waterlogged throughout the growing season, allowing the compost surface to dry out slightly between waterings. Feed every two weeks with a general liquid houseplant fertilizer when the plant is actively growing and once or twice during the winter.

PESTS AND PROBLEMS

Aphids, mealy bugs and red spider mite can affect *Cissus.* Brown blotches on the leaves and leaf loss result from excessive sunlight. When plants are underwatered, the lower leaves become brown-spotted and curl. If temperatures are too low, the leaves wilt and if they fall, it may be the result of over or underwatering or too much sunshine. Underfeeding causes slow growth.

LONGEVITY

With proper care, this is a long-lived plant in the home.

Right: Cissus rhombifolia *creates an elegant display when trained up canes, with the tendrils providing some support. The delicate new growth is covered in fine silvery hairs.*

Above: Cissus rhombifolia *'Ellen Danica', a form with deeply lobed leaflets, is a justifiably popular houseplant that looks especially effective planted in a hanging container. It is prone to powdery mildew, so do not let the compost in the pot dry out too much.*

Left: Cissus *'Jubilee' produces masses of glossy foliage, which can be allowed to trail or be trained up a suitable support to produce an impressive display.*

CLIVIA

This dark handsome plant from the dry forests of South Africa displays its elegant, arching, glossy leaves throughout the year. The foliage provides a perfect contrast for the clusters of orange, bell-shaped flowers and the shining red berries. Clivias flower better when they are potbound and should only be repotted when the roots are bursting from the pot.

Kaffir lilies need bright light for healthy growth and flower production. If light levels are too low, no flowers will be produced, and in direct sunshine the leaves become yellow and scorched. During the growing season, moderate temperatures are needed but over winter, during their resting period, plants can be put in a cool room. They dislike high temperatures at any time, but tolerate dry air, so misting is not necessary. Clivias flower better when they are potbound and dislike root disturbance, so if you tease out the roots when repotting they will stop flowering for a year or two. Repot every four to six years after flowering when the plant is eventually forced out of the pot by its roots.

In the years when they are not repotted, topdress the plants in late winter by carefully removing the top 5cm of compost and replacing it with fresh mixture. Use a peat substitute-based potting compost as used for repotting. If you have space, you can achieve a larger, more impressive display by not dividing the plant or removing the offsets and allowing it to develop into a huge clump.

Wipe the leaves regularly with a soft damp cloth to remove dust and when the blooms have faded, in late spring to early summer, remove them and wait for the stem to die down before removing it, too. If you would like to try growing clivias from seed, leave the fruits to ripen. Contrary to popular belief, this does not usually prevent the plant from flowering in the following years.

PROPAGATION

Divide plants or remove offsets when repotting. Remove the plant from the pot, gently tease away the compost, pull or ease the sections apart and pot them singly into 10-13cm pots of peat substitute-based potting compost, just burying the base of the stems. Water thoroughly with tepid water. Stand them in a warm place. It may take two to three years before the plant is established and flowers again. Repot as normal.

Fruits are produced after flowering and take a year to turn red and ripen. When they begin to soften, carefully remove the pale brown seeds and plant them about 6mm deep in seed compost in 7.5cm pots. Keep them warm and moist on a windowsill or in a propagator. Germination takes anything up to three months or more. Pot on into 13cm pots only when necessary. It could be four years or more before the plants produce any flowers; these will be produced in varying shades of orange.

Right: *The green-tipped orange flowers of* Clivia nobilis, *displayed just above the arching foliage, are not flamboyant but certainly striking and unusual.*

FEEDING AND WATERING

Feed and water well, using tepid water. Keep the compost moist during the growing season, allowing the surface to dry out between waterings. Gradually reduce watering in the autumn and keep the plants almost dry from late autumn to early winter. Allow the top half of the compost to dry out before rewatering thoroughly. Check moisture content by pushing your finger into the compost. If crumbs are attached to your finger, the compost is moist; if not, it is dry. In spring, when the flower spike is 10-15cm tall, gradually increase watering. Feed with a liquid flowering houseplant fertilizer from spring to autumn and once or twice in winter if the plant is in warm conditions.

PESTS AND PROBLEMS

Mealy bug and scale may be a problem. If the resting period is too short, the room too warm or light levels too low, flowers may not appear. The flowers will not last long if there is too much warmth.

LONGEVITY

With an adequate rest period, clivias last for many years.

Kaffir lily

Other varieties of interest
C. miniata var. *citrina*: Beautiful pale lemon flowers.

Left: *Clivia miniata has a stiff flowering stem topped with a cluster of ostentatious orange flowers. The overlapping dark green leaves form a a distinctive feature too.*

Below: *Clivia miniata 'Striata', a sensational combination of orange flowers and variegated leaves with a 'painted' look.*

Repotting clivias
Remove the plant carefully from its pot, insert the pot into another, one size larger and using it as a template, firm compost into the gap between the two pots. Carefully remove the inner pot and slide the rootball of the clivia into the space. Add compost to cover the exposed roots and leave sufficient space between the mixture and the rim of the pot to allow room for watering. Soak with tepid water. By repotting in this way, the rootball is barely disturbed and the plant should flower again the following season. Clay pots provide stability for larger plants, which can become top heavy.

CODIAEUM

Could Joseph's coat have been as dazzlingly coloured and boldly patterned as the glossy leaves of this magnificent shrub? Resplendent in a multitude of vibrant shades, including yellow, orange and red, such is the variety of leaf shape and colour that no one leaf matches another. A common garden plant in the tropics, *Codiaeum* brings a warming glow to houses in cooler climates.

Constant bright light throughout the year is vital to maintain good leaf colour, so in winter, when light levels are low, the leaves may fade a little. The plants prefer moderate to warm room conditions throughout the year, but tolerate lower winter temperatures if the compost is kept almost dry. They dislike fluctuating temperatures and draughts. Humidity is important, too, so mist your plants regularly with tepid water, group them together or stand them on a shallow tray of pebbles filled with water to just below the base of the pot. Wiping the leaves regularly with a damp cloth removes dust and helps to maintain humidity.

If the compost is congested with roots, repot plants into pots one size larger each spring, using John Innes No. 2 compost, and water them in thoroughly. Once the maximum convenient pot size is reached, topdress the plants annually by carefully removing and replacing the top 5cm of compost. Pinch out the growing tips of young plants to encourage bushy growth. Prune where necessary in early spring to maintain the shape of the plant, and regenerate older, spindly specimens by cutting them back to within a few centimetres of the base. Water sparingly at first, increasing the amount as they regrow; you can use the shoots that you remove as cuttings. Growing several cuttings in one pot creates a spectacular display. Wear gloves when pruning and propagating and do not rub your eyes or mouth, as the sap is an irritant.

1

2

PROPAGATION

Propagate *Codiaeum* in spring, using a 7.5cm-long tip from a healthy side shoot on the current season's growth.

1 *Trim with a sharp knife just below the leaf joint and remove the basal leaves. Cut surfaces bleed white sap; to stop the bleeding, spray the cutting with water, dip it in powdered charcoal or push the cut surface into compost to cap the end.*

2 *Using a pencil or thin cane, make a hole a few centimetres deep in a 7.5cm pot of moist cutting compost. If the leaves are large, cut them in half. Dip the base of the cutting in hormone rooting powder, gently tapping off the excess. Insert the cutting and firm the compost gently around the stem. Place the pot in a loosely knotted plastic bag supported by four canes and put it in a warm, bright position. After four to six weeks, when the roots have formed and the cutting begins to grow, remove the plastic bag. Allow the cutting to acclimatize for about a week and then pot it on as necessary.*

FEEDING AND WATERING

When plants are actively growing, keep the compost moist but avoid waterlogging. Water sparingly in lower temperatures, allowing the compost surface to dry out between waterings. Feed the plants every two weeks during the growing season, using a liquid fertilizer for foliage houseplants. Do not feed in winter.

PESTS AND PROBLEMS

Red spider mite, scale insect and mealy bug may be a problem with these plants.

Lower leaves are lost as a result of draughts, dry compost, low humidity and low temperatures.

Fading leaf colour is caused by lack of light, so move plants to a brighter position. Scorched, brittle leaf tips and margins are caused by dry air; keep plants away from radiators and increase the humidity around them.

LONGEVITY

In good growing conditions codiaeums should last for many years.

OTHER VARIETIES OF INTEREST

Codiaeum variegatum var. *pictum* 'Carrierei': Yellow-green leaves when young, maturing to dark green with a red centre.

C.v.p. 'Disraeli': Mid-green leaves, heavily blotched with cream and yellow above, flushed red beneath.

C.v.p. 'Spirale': Narrow, multicoloured leaves in combinations of green, red and yellow and twisted like a corkscrew.

Codiaeum 'Excellent': Attractively shaped leaves in exuberant tones.

Codiaeum 'Gold Finger' and 'Gold Sun': Both variations on the theme of 'Gold Star'.

Above: *The leaves of* Codiaeum *'Goldstar' look as if they have been splashed with yellow paint. A superb plant for a vividly coloured room.*

Below: *The undulating leaves of* C. *'Red Curl' may not be to everyone's taste, but they are very unusual and guaranteed to cause comment.*

Right: *The brightly veined leaves of* C. variegatum *'Petra' are an instant eye-catcher and add a touch of cheer to any room.*

GOLDFISH PLANT

COLUMNEA

These exotic-looking plants are not as difficult to grow as their appearance suggests. Their elegant stems and green leaves look wonderful cascading over the top of a pot, and spectacular, vivid orange flowers appear like shoals of goldfish swimming among the dark green glossy foliage. A winter rest will encourage a greater profusion of flowers.

To grow successfully, columneas need bright light, but not scorching sunshine, throughout the year. Constant moderate temperatures during the growing season and a draught-free position are also vital for healthy growth and plentiful flowers. Perhaps most surprisingly for a tropical plant, columneas appreciate a rest at slightly lower temperatures from early winter until spring. Water them sparingly at this time so that the roots do not rot. Columneas dislike hot dry air and need constant humidity. As the leaves are prone to scorch if misted in bright light, it is better to provide humidity by grouping plants together or by standing them on a shallow tray of pebbles filled with water to just below the base of the pot.

Every two years in late spring or when the roots fill the pot, repot columneas into shallow containers one size larger, using a mix of peat-substitute compost with added coarse sand, perlite, polystyrene granules or grit. Alternatively, trim back the roots to about two thirds of their original length, repot the plants into the same container using fresh compost and water thoroughly. Older plants eventually become straggly, and can be pruned back to within a few centimetres of the base after flowering or during the spring. Remove any dead or weak shoots and faded flowers as soon as you see them.

PROPAGATION
Propagate columneas from healthy 7.5cm-long shoot tips after flowering.

1. *Trim with a sharp knife just below the leaf joint and remove the basal leaves.*
2. *Make four holes a few centimetres deep in a 7.5cm pot of moist cutting mixture. Dip the base of the cuttings in hormone rooting powder, gently tapping off the excess. Insert the cuttings and firm the compost gently around the stems. Place the pot in a loosely knotted plastic bag, supported by four canes, and put it in a warm spot away from direct light. Rooting takes about four weeks. Once roots are formed and the cuttings begin to grow, remove the bag to acclimatize them for about a week and then put them in their final position. Pinch out growing tips to encourage bushiness. For a dense display, transfer three or four rooted cuttings into a 25-30cm pot.*

FEEDING AND WATERING
Avoid waterlogging. Using tepid water, keep the compost moist during the growing season, allowing the surface to dry out between waterings in winter. Stand columneas on a pedestal or tall table so that you can water them easily and correctly. Either plunge the pot into a bucket of water for half an hour or soak the compost using a watering can. Take particular care with those in hanging containers to ensure that they are properly drained before rehanging. Alternatively, stand the pot in a larger hanging container and empty out the excess after watering.

Feed with liquid flowering houseplant fertilizer every two weeks in summer and every four weeks in winter.

PESTS AND PROBLEMS
Aphids and grey mould can be a problem for columneas.

Leaf drop can occur if the air is too dry or warm. Water on the leaves can cause unsightly scorching if the light levels are too high.

LONGEVITY
With care, columneas last for many years in the home.

***Right:** The flat bushy habit of* Columnea *'Wilde Brand' is dotted with clusters of stunning tubular flowers. A worthwhile plant indeed!*

***Below:** The dark foliage of* Columnea *'Apollo' is the ideal backcloth for its pale yellow and bright orange flowers.*

Left: Columnea *'Sanne'. The orange-red flowers seem to leap out from the foliage in this stiff-stemmed variety.*

CORDYLINE

These handsome, slow-growing foliage plants from the tropical rainforests of Southeast Asia and Polynesia make spectacular single specimens, and when several are grouped together their impact is an exploding kaleidoscope of colour. *Cordyline fruticosa* and other varieties are ideal for a warm bathroom or kitchen where humidity is high. They propagate readily from sections of stem.

To maintain strong leaf coloration, and vigorous growth, cordylines need bright light, but not scorching sunshine, and constantly warm conditions away from draughts. They will, however, tolerate moderate winter temperatures if watering is reduced. Another vital factor for good growth is high humidity, so mist plants regularly using tepid water, group them together or place them on a shallow tray of pebbles filled with water to just below the base of the pot. Keep the leaves dust-free by wiping them with a moist cloth to maintain humidity.

Every two to three years, when the compost becomes congested with roots, repot plants in spring into pots one size larger, using peat substitute-based compost. Water thoroughly with tepid water. Once you have repotted plants to the maximum convenient pot size, topdress them annually by carefully removing and replacing the top 5-7.5cm of compost.

Older plants naturally lose their lower leaves but can be revitalized by pruning back the main stem in spring or early summer to within a few centimetres of the base. This encourages the production of new shoots that will form a bushier plant. You can use the old stem for cuttings.

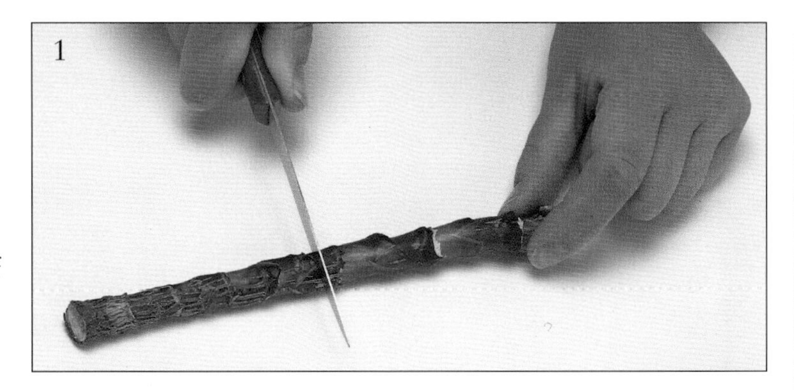
1

2

3

PROPAGATION

They are easy to propagate from stem sections. Pruning may provide plenty of material.

1 *Cut the stems of old leggy plants into 7.5cm sections in late spring.*

2 *Insert the pieces vertically into pots, almost burying them in cutting compost.*

3 *Place in a plastic bag and keep in a warm room. When top growth appears, pot cuttings singly into 7.5-10cm pots of peat substitute-based compost or John Innes No 2. Pot on as they increase in size. The first leaves are usually green; coloured foliage appears after about one or two years.*

FEEDING AND WATERING

During active growth, keep the compost moist but never waterlogged. Allow the compost surface to dry out between waterings. Keep it slightly moist in winter, but take care not to overwater, particularly at lower temperatures. During late spring to early autumn, feed every two weeks with a liquid fertilizer suitable for foliage plants, but feed only once a month during winter.

PESTS AND PROBLEMS

Cordylines are generally free from pests, but occasionally suffer from aphids and red spider mite.

Low light levels, low temperatures or dry air cause browning of the leaf tips and margins. Direct sunshine causes scorching and brown patches on the leaves.

LONGEVITY

Under good growing conditions, plants last for several years.

Ti plant

***Right:** The leaves of* Cordyline fruticosa *'Kiwi' are attractively marked in red, lime and dark green. This striking plant would add a touch of the tropics to any room.*

Left: Cordyline fruticosa *'Lord Robertson' has an aristocratic aura that goes with the name. Its dark green leaves with slender red margins would look perfect in a richly decorated room.*

Right: Cordyline fruticosa *'Red Edge' is a compact plant with broad pink margins that sometimes threaten to spread over the whole leaf.*

Other varieties of interest

C.f. 'Atoom': Has dark green leaves splashed red.
C.f. 'Baby Ti': A small plant with red leaf margins.
C. australis and its cultivars can be grown indoors while small and will survive outdoors in summer. They need a lot of space to grow.

CYCLAMEN

The cyclamen is undoubtedly one of the most popular winter-flowering houseplants, available in a spectacular choice of flower colour and plant sizes from miniature to standard. Its delicate, swept-back flowers with slightly twisted petals are displayed on dainty stems above deep green leaves, patterned in silvery grey. Although cyclamen are often disposed of after flowering, they are easy to keep for succeeding years.

When cyclamen are growing and flowering they need good light; a bright windowsill is an ideal spot. They need, but rarely receive, the cool, airy conditions found in an unheated room, but if temperatures are too low, they stop flowering. Most plants are kept in centrally heated rooms and soon become spindly, their leaves turn yellow and the flowers fall. A spot on a windowsill above a radiator ensures their rapid demise. In cold, humid conditions or if air circulation is poor, grey mould appears as a fluffy growth on flowers and buds. Humidity is important, so stand the plant on a tray of pebbles filled with water to just below the base of the pot, and occasionally mist around the pot, taking care not to wet the flowers. Remove fading flowers and their stalks and damaged or yellowing leaves. Yellowing foliage is usually caused by high temperatures and dry air, but check that they have not been overwatered or exposed to direct sunlight.

It is very easy to persuade plants to flower in successive years. In good growing conditions, a cyclamen remains in growth until late spring. As fewer flowers appear and the leaves begin to turn yellow, carefully pull away the dying leaves. Once more than half the leaves have yellowed, stop watering the plant and remove the dead leaves. As it is perfectly happy outdoors in the summer, leave the plant in its pot in a sunny position and allow it to bake in the sunshine. Turn the pot on its side so that the compost does not become waterlogged after summer rain, causing the tuber to rot. From mid- to late summer, check it regularly for signs of growth and immediately they appear, begin watering, sparingly at first and increasing the amount as more growth appears. Once the first leaves have established, begin feeding. Bring the plant indoors to a cool room before the first frosts. Continue feeding and watering until there is sufficient growth to put the cyclamen on display.

Below: *Soak the seeds for about 24 hours before planting and keep the compost moist by watering the tray with tepid water from below.*

PROPAGATION

Cyclamen can be grown from freshly collected seed, but the offspring will look different to the parents. Moisten the seed compost, scatter the seeds over the surface 2-3cm apart and cover with a thin layer of compost. Put in a warm, shady spot to germinate. When two leaves appear, pot seedlings in a mix as for adult plants.

REPOTTING

Repot plants after three or four years, as they flower better when slightly potbound. Do this when the first growths appear and use a peat substitute-based compost with added sharp sand. Bury the tuber to half its depth and water sparingly.

FEEDING AND WATERING

Keep the compost moist with soft tepid water while the plant is actively growing, allowing the surface to dry slightly between waterings. Do not wet the centre of the plant or the tuber will rot. Water from below and drain off the excess after an hour. When the plant is in flower, feed every three weeks with a liquid flowering houseplant fertilizer; in spring, feed every two weeks with a general liquid houseplant fertilizer.

PESTS AND PROBLEMS

Cyclamen mite causes new growth to distort. Leaf margins become thickened and curl, flowers die, buds twist and the stems distort. There is no control available, so destroy plants immediately.

Plants collapse and die when attacked by vine weevil. Empty out the compost and if you find cream-coloured larvae with brown heads, squash them immediately and dispose of the plant.

LONGEVITY

Plants can last for several years and older, larger specimens are magnificent in foliage and flower.

***Left:** The 'mini' cyclamen 'Anneli' is only about 15cm tall and makes an ideal novelty plant that children would enjoy growing.*

VARIETIES OF INTEREST

Standard varieties: A range of cyclamen that grow to 30cm tall in a variety of colours. Some have fringed petals and double flowers.

Intermediate varieties: These cyclamen grow to about 25cm. They are compact and floriferous.

Miniature varieties: These are about 15cm tall with small leaves and flowers in a range of colours.

***Below:** The exquisite flowers of cyclamen are an absolute joy. These white-margined pink petals shade to a darker centre.*

***Right:** Wine-red blooms stand above a mass of boldly marked leaves in this lovely cyclamen cultivar. Such a display brings welcome colour to the house in winter.*

CYPERUS

This tropical waterside plant has wonderful foliage, erect stems, a graceful habit and is crowned with flower heads like the spokes of an open umbrella. Being naturally at home in damp conditions, it needs constantly moist compost and perhaps its greatest attraction is that it is impossible to overwater. It is easy to grow, simple to propagate and an excellent plant for beginners.

The aptly named umbrella plant, *Cyperus involucratus (alternifolius)*, prefers bright light but tolerates some direct sunshine, light shade or even poor light for short periods. It thrives in moderate to warm conditions and should not be subjected to low temperatures. High humidity is important, particularly during the summer or in centrally heated homes in winter, so mist your plants regularly with tepid water, group plants together or stand them in a shallow tray of water, which also serves as a watering reservoir. Repot plants annually in spring or immediately the stems fill their present pot. Use John Innes No. 2 in a container one size larger and water thoroughly. Pot young plants in John Innes No. 1, which contains less fertilizer. They need little care apart from removing old stems, which turn yellow.

3

Roots emerge from the tip of the upturned umbrella and a small new plant appears and grows upwards.

1

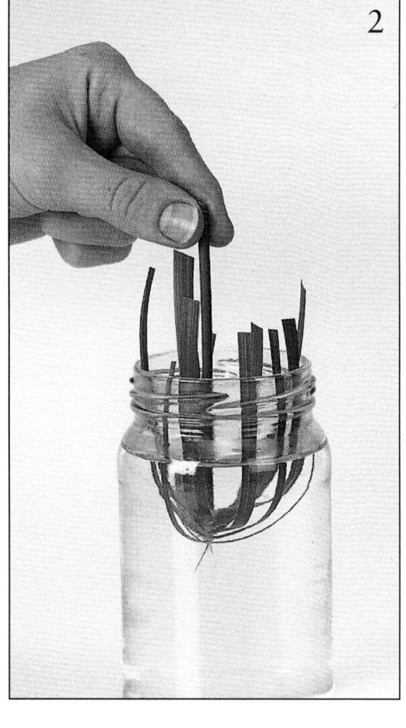

2

PROPAGATION

The method imitates the natural process in the plant's aquatic habitat. The stems bend down towards the water and roots form at the centre of the 'umbrella', which detaches as the parent stem rots away.

1 Cut off an umbrella.
2 Upturn and plunge it head first into a bottle or jar of tepid water. Keep it in a light spot and roots will develop on the flower head.
3 Eventually a young plant will form an umbrella and grow upwards. Carefully pot the new plant and move it into bright light to establish.

FEEDING AND WATERING

Cyperus are perfectly happy to stand permanently in a shallow tray of tepid water, which keeps the compost moist. If you are the sort of person who forgets to water their plants, this is the one for you. During active growth, feed every two weeks with a general liquid fertilizer. Feed once or twice in winter.

PESTS AND PROBLEMS

Cyperus may suffer from mealy bug. Check plants regularly as small populations are easier to eradicate. Isolate affected plants.

Browning of the leaf tips and margins is usually caused by dry air or drying out of the compost; increase humidity and water. In low light levels there is little new growth.

The 'umbrellas' turn yellow and wither if the compost is allowed to dry out. Cut off the affected stems at the base, water thoroughly and leave the pot standing in shallow water.

LONGEVITY

As umbrella plants are easily repropagated and fast-growing, material from one plant will last for many years.

OTHER VARIETIES OF INTEREST

Cyperus involucratus 'Gracilis': A dwarf variety to 30cm tall.

C. i. 'Variegatus': White-striped leaves and stems.

C. i. 'Nanus': Dwarf form.

Cyperus longus: A robust plant of variable height that may reach 150cm tall. Leaves and stems are a glossy green.

Cyperus papyrus: Needs warmth and humidity. Stand pot in a shallow tray of water. A challenge to grow.

C. p. 'Nanus': Dwarf form.

Below: Cyperus cyperoides *is a dense plant with long, elegant flower heads. Sometimes seen as* C. sumula *or* C. alternifolius *'Zumula'.*

Above: Cyperus albostriatus *(sometimes seen as* C. diffusus*) is compact and does not usually need staking. This type has pale green leaves and stems.*

Right: Cyperus involucratus *produces dense clusters of elegant stems that usually need staking. Can grow to 90-120cm tall.*

DIEFFENBACHIA

These deservedly popular houseplants have an imposing presence, either as single specimens or as a feature in mixed displays. Their canelike stems support slightly arching leaves of rare brilliance, boldly variegated and speckled or splashed with colour, which makes them impossible to ignore. Although lower leaves are lost with age, pruning provides cuttings and regenerates the plant.

Dieffenbachias like bright light all year, with some shade in summer. If the levels are too high or low the variegation fades. Conditions should be warm to moderate. In winter, the plants will survive for short periods in cool conditions if the compost is almost dry; if it remains too cool for too long, the lower leaves are likely to turn yellow, wilt and then fall. Avoid draughts and fluctuating temperatures at all costs and maintain a constantly humid atmosphere. Draughts and dry air stunt growth and cause yellow and brown patches on the leaves, while dry compost or hot, dry or cold air causes browning of the leaf tips and margins. Wiping the leaves also maintains humidity and helps to keep them dust-free. Repot dieffenbachias each year in spring or when the roots start to grow through the base of the pot. Use a pot one size larger, a peat substitute-based compost and water thoroughly. Pot on each year until your plants are in 30cm pots and in future years topdress in spring by replacing the top 5-7.5cm of compost.

The lower leaves of older plants naturally dry up and can be carefully pulled off. For a while the bare stem is hidden by the arching leaves, but when it becomes conspicuous, cut back the main stem to 5-7.5cm in spring, keep the compost slightly moist and increase watering when the plant resprouts.

PROPAGATION

From mid-spring to early summer, take healthy 7.5-10cm-long shoot tips from the current season's growth or a daughter plant from the base.

1 *Trim with a sharp knife just below a leaf joint and remove the basal leaves.*
2 *Dip the base of the cutting in hormone rooting powder, tapping off the excess. Insert and firm the moist compost around the stem.*
3 *Place the pot in a loosely knotted plastic bag, supported by four canes, and put it in a warm spot away from direct light. Once roots are formed and the cutting begins to grow, remove the bag, allow it to acclimatize for about a week and then transfer into a separate 7.5-10cm pot. Pot on as the plant increases in size, using compost for mature plants.*

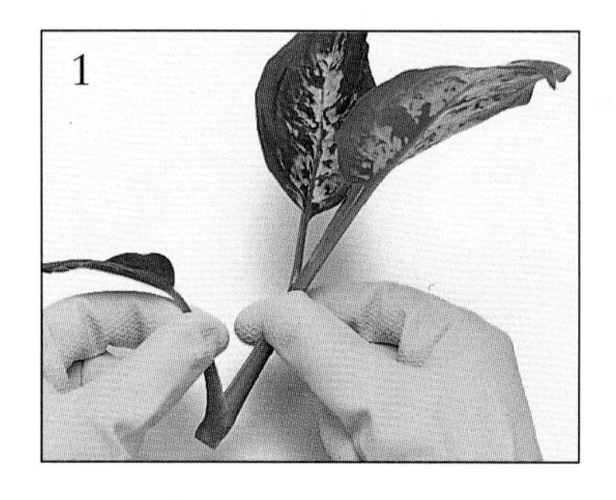
1

2

3

FEEDING AND WATERING

Using tepid water, keep the compost moist, not water-logged and allow the surface to dry out slightly between each watering. Water sparingly in low winter temperatures. In warm conditions, plants will continue to grow throughout the year and should remain constantly moist. Feed with a liquid fertilizer for foliage houseplants once every two weeks in summer and every four weeks in winter.

PESTS AND PROBLEMS

Dieffenbachias are usually trouble-free, but may suffer from scale, aphids and red spider mite if it is too dry.

If the base of the stem becomes soft and discoloured, this is a sign of stem rot, a condition encouraged by overwatering and low temperatures. If the damage is slight, cut out the diseased area, spray with fungicide and repot. If the damage is severe, discard the plant and use the top as a cutting.

LONGEVITY

Given favourable conditions, dieffenbachias can last for several years.

HANDLE WITH CARE

It is important to note that all parts of *Dieffenbachia* are poisonous, so wear gloves when taking cuttings or pruning. Take care not to wipe your eyes or mouth and wash your hands after handling the plants. However, do not let this discourage you from growing these wonderful plants.

Left: *D. seguine 'Tropic Snow'. The dark green of the leaves and stems contrasts with the cream and pale green centre.*

Right: *The bright lemon-cream leaves and dark margins of D. 'Camilla' create an outstanding contrast.*

Below right: *D. 'Veerle Compacta' has a dense growth habit and is less inclined to become spindly as the plant matures. It has exquisite colours and markings.*

OTHER VARIETIES OF INTEREST

D. x *bausei*: Long leaves to 30cm or more, pale yellow flushed with green and marked with white-and-cream spots and blotches.
D. 'Exotica': The small leaves are variably patterned with cream-and-yellow variegation on a dark green background.
D. 'Tropic Sun': Has green margins and is patterned with yellow-green and cream markings.
D. seguine 'Maculata': Long, narrow, white-spotted leaves.

DRACAENA

If you are looking for plants with bold, dramatic foliage in a variety of colours, it is worth considering dracaenas. They are now one of the most popular indoor foliage plants, as their striking leaves make such a wonderfully bold statement. As young plants they can be displayed on a table or shelf, but when mature they are large enough to dominate a corner of any room.

Because dracaenas come from tropical Africa, they like to be kept warm and draught-free all year round. If temperatures are too low over a long period, the leaves will droop and fall, but the plants can tolerate occasional low temperatures. Dracaenas are most likely to survive a chill if the compost is only slightly moist. Keep them in bright light away from scorching sunlight, which damages the leaves; too little light causes leaves to lose colour and stop growing. *Dracaena marginata* is the most robust, tolerating some shade and cool winter conditions. All dracaenas like humid conditions, so group them with other plants, spray them with tepid water or stand the pot on a tray of pebbles half-filled with water.

Grow dracaenas in John Innes No. 2 compost and check the root growth every year by carefully easing the rootball from the pot. Repot if necessary in spring when the pot becomes congested with roots. Well-cared-for, mature dracaenas make fine specimen plants. Cleaning the leaves with a soft, damp cloth keeps them dust-free and better able to use the light. Support each leaf with the back of your hand and wipe it gently.

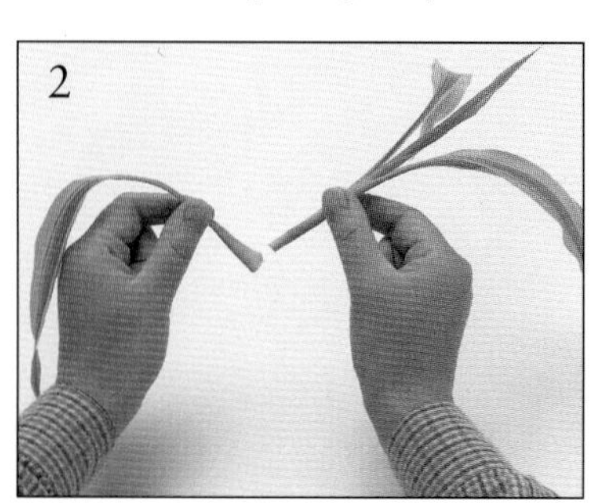

PROPAGATION
Propagate by tip cuttings

1 *Take a healthy tip cutting.*
2 *Remove the basal leaves.*
3 *Make a shallow hole in a pot of moist cutting compost. Dip the base in hormone rooting powder, tap off the excess and plant the cutting.*
4 *Put the pot in a plastic bag and keep it in a warm spot away from direct light.*

You can take stem cuttings after pruning. Cut the central part of the stem into 5-7.5cm sections, each with a bud swelling. Press the pieces horizontally into peat substitute-based compost and secure with a piece of bent wire. Moisten the compost and cover with a plastic bag.

FEEDING AND WATERING
In the growing season, keep the soil moist using tepid water and allow the surface to dry between waterings. Apply a general houseplant fertilizer every two weeks. If plants are overwintered in cooler conditions, reduce watering and only feed every two months.

PESTS AND PROBLEMS
Aphids and mealy bugs can be a problem. Dry air or cold draughts can cause the leaf tips to brown and margins to turn yellow. Yellowing lower leaves occur naturally; these droop and are eventually shed.

LONGEVITY
Dracaenas are long-lived, yet rarely seen at their full height, because once the bare stems become obvious, they are usually cut back to within about 30cm of the base and used for cuttings. When cut back, dracaenas send out new shoots and produce an even better display. Reduce watering until new growth appears.

Left: Dracaena marginata *'Tricolor' has yellow, red and green leaves clustered at the top of its elegant stems. It is an ideal specimen plant and one of the most tolerant dracaenas.*

Right: D. fragrans *'Massangeana' has a yellow central stripe. Group other plants around the base of tall dracaenas to mask the leafless stems.*

Left: The distinctive leaf colours of D. deremensis *'Green Stripe' make it an excellent specimen plant. Choose colours that complement the decor of your room.*

OTHER VARIETIES OF INTEREST

D. deremensis 'Janet Craig': Dark green undulating leaves.
D. d. 'Lemon and Lime': Lime green leaves with dark green centres are edged with white. *D. d.* 'Yellow Stripe' and 'White Stripe': Yellow and white margins.
D. fragrans 'Lindenii': Leaves have bold cream-coloured margins.
D. marginata 'Colorama': Green-and-yellow striped with bold red stripes on leaf margins.

DEVIL'S IVY

EPIPREMNUM

You would hardly recognize the rampant climber draping its golden cloak of giant leaves over trees in tropical gardens as the plant you have at home. Thankfully, it is more restrained, and the juvenile form with heart-shaped leaves is a most attractive houseplant. It can be trained up moss poles, trellis or wires, yet trails elegantly from hanging baskets or from a pot on a plinth.

PROPAGATION

You will find that as with many houseplants, devil's ivy is easy to propagate. Why not take several cuttings and give them to your friends and family.

1 *Take a healthy 7.5-10cm-long shoot tip from the current season's growth. Trim it with a sharp knife just below the leaf joint and remove the basal leaves.*
2 *Using a thin cane, make a hole a few centimetres deep in a 9cm pot of moist cutting compost. Dip the base of the cutting in hormone rooting powder, gently tapping off the excess. Insert the cutting and firm the compost gently around the stem.*
3 *Place the pot in a loosely knotted plastic bag supported by four canes and put it in a warm position away from direct sunlight. Once roots are formed and the cutting begins to grow, remove the bag, allow it to acclimatize for about a week and pot it on.*

Cuttings of *Epipremnum* also root easily in water.

Bright light, away from scorching sunshine, is ideal for devil's ivy and keeps the leaf coloration strong. At low light levels, the leaves become smaller and their colour fades. Draughts or sudden drops in temperature cause the leaves to curl and become limp, so provide constant moderate temperatures when the plant is actively growing, and give it a rest in a cool room in winter. Mist plants occasionally with tepid water, more often if temperatures rise. Stand smaller plants on a tray of pebbles half-filled with water.

When the pot becomes congested with roots, repot plants in spring into a pot one size larger using John Innes No.2 and water thoroughly. Once the maximum pot size is reached, topdress plants annually by carefully removing and replacing the top 5-7.5cm of compost. Prune back any stems that have outgrown their allotted space in spring to just above a healthy leaf. New shoots will soon appear and you can use the prunings for cuttings. Wipe the leaves regularly with a soft damp cloth to remove dust.

FEEDING AND WATERING

Keep the compost moist with tepid water, allowing the surface to dry out between each watering. At lower winter temperatures, give the plant just enough water to prevent wilting. Beware of overwatering.

Feed every three weeks in summer with a general liquid houseplant fertilizer and once or twice in winter.

PESTS AND PROBLEMS

Dry air or underwatering can cause brown patches on the leaf and its margins; increase watering and humidity.

Rotting stems and yellowing, falling leaves are usually caused by over-watering. Stop watering and allow the compost surface to dry out; water moderately.

If there is insufficient light, leaves revert to green.

LONGEVITY

When displayed with several plants growing around the edge of a hanging basket, they should last for two or three years. After that, replace them with newly rooted cuttings and fresh compost. Single plants in large pots can last for many years.

Above: *The lime-green leaves of* Epipremnum *'Neon' create a really eye-catching display.*

Below: Epipremnum *'Marble Queen'. This unusual variety, with white leaf stems and attractively marbled foliage, needs constant bright light. It is less vigorous than* E. aureum.

Above: *The best way to appreciate the long stems and variegated leaves of* E. aureum *is to see them tumbling down from a hanging container.*

EUPHORBIA PULCHERRIMA

It is hard to imagine that *Euphorbia pulcherrima*, a compact, bushy, pot plant with an insignificant central cluster of tiny flowers and magnificent coloured bracts, becomes a large bush or small tree in Mediterranean or tropical gardens. The bracts can last for several months; choose a plant with unopened flowers for a long-lasting display and protect it from cold on the journey home.

Poinsettias need a bright position in constant, moderate temperatures away from draughts. To keep humidity high, lightly mist plants with soft tepid water or stand them on a tray of pebbles filled with water to just below the base of the pot.

Although they are usually discarded when the bracts begin to fade, you can persuade poinsettias to flower the following year. In late spring, reduce watering and once the leaves wither and fall, keep the compost dry for three to four weeks. After this resting period, take a pair of sharp secateurs, cut back the main stems to 5-8cm and soak the compost thoroughly to encourage new shoots to develop. When they appear, replant the poinsettia into the same pot or one slightly larger, using peat-substitute compost, and place it in a bright, warm position. Water regularly, allowing the compost surface to dry out between waterings, and feed every two weeks with a general liquid fertilizer. As they grow, thin out the stems, leaving the strongest four or five. The challenge is to have bracts in full colour for Christmas. As poinsettias will only initiate flowers and bracts when the hours of daylight are short, give plants fourteen hours of complete darkness every night for eight weeks from the beginning of September by putting them in a dark cupboard or covering the plants with a thick black plastic bag or bin liner. You can then return them to their original position. Plants grown on for successive years are larger than the original plant, as nurseries either treat plants with a growth retardant or subject them to a temperature regime that encourages compact, bushy plants to develop.

1

2

PROPAGATION

When pruning back the new growth to the strongest four or five stems, use the most vigorous as tip cuttings.

1 *In late spring to early summer, take healthy shoot tips about 7.5cm long. Trim them with a sharp knife just below a leaf joint and remove the basal leaves.*

2 *Using a cane, make holes a few centimetres deep in a 9cm pot of moist cutting compost. Dip the base of the cuttings in water to help the hormone rooting powder adhere to the cut, then dip them in the powder, gently tapping off the excess. Insert the cuttings and firm the compost gently around the stem. Place the pot in a loosely knotted plastic bag, supported by four canes, and put it in a warm, bright position, away from direct sunlight. Once the cuttings begin to grow, remove the bag, allow them to acclimatize for about a week and then stand them in a suitable position. Pot on the cuttings as required and pinch out the growing tips for a bushy plant.*

FEEDING AND WATERING

Keep the compost moist using tepid water, allowing the surface to dry out before rewatering. If you plan to keep the plant for the following year, feed it monthly when on display with a liquid houseplant fertilizer. Plants kept for one season need no feeding.

PESTS AND PROBLEMS

Red spider mite and mealy bug may affect plants. In dry air, the coloured bracts and leaf margins become brown and fall; keep the surrounding air moist. Low temperatures, draughts and overwatering cause the leaves to curl, wilt, turn yellow and fall.

LONGEVITY

As plants are cheap and freely available, they are usually replaced annually. Those that are kept can be grown on for several years.

HANDLE WITH CARE

Poinsettia sap is poisonous and can cause skin irritation, so it is a good idea to wear gloves when handling plants and taking cuttings.

Poinsettia

Left: *As single specimen plants, white poinsettias make a focal point in any room.*

Below: *The red poinsettia is traditionally associated with Christmas displays.*

Above and below: *Although poinsettias are traditionally red, a wider range of colours is now available. Look out for varieties with pink bracts or flushed pink or variegated bracts. They make a subtle yet attractive display that lasts for many weeks.*

FATSIA

The warm, humid, seaside woodlands of Japan, Taiwan and their smaller surrounding islands are the natural home of *Fatsia japonica*. However, this is a wonderfully resilient specimen plant that tolerates temperatures almost down to freezing, although it dislikes dry air and high temperatures. Its glossy, stiff, dark green leaves mass together to create a bold and dramatic architectural effect.

Although *Fatsia* prefers bright light, particularly in winter, it tolerates some shade and enjoys cool to moderate temperatures. With careful winter watering, it will survive temperatures almost down to freezing and can spend the summer outdoors when there is no danger of frost. It prefers high humidity, so mist plants regularly, stand them on pebbles in a shallow tray filled with water to just below the base of the pot or group several plants together. Cut back the tips of young plants to encourage bushy growth and wipe the leaves occasionally with a damp cloth to remove dust. If the compost is congested with roots, repot plants in spring, into a pot one size larger containing John Innes No 2 or a peat-substitute compost. Once plants have reached the maximum convenient pot size, remove and replace the top 5-7.5cm of compost each year and replace the compost every two years. After repotting, water plants thoroughly.

1

PROPAGATION

Take a healthy 7.5-10cm-long shoot tip from the current season's growth in summer.

1 *Trim with a sharp knife just below the leaf joint and remove the basal leaves.*
2 *Make a shallow hole in a 9cm pot of moist cutting compost. Dip the base of the cutting in hormone rooting powder, gently tap off the excess, insert the cutting and firm it in gently.*
3 *Place the pot in a loosely knotted plastic bag, supported by four canes, and put it in a warm corner away from direct light.*

2

3

FEEDING AND WATERING

Water regularly from spring to autumn, allowing the compost surface to dry out between watering. Water sparingly in winter. Do not allow the compost to become waterlogged. Feed every two weeks in summer with a general liquid fertilizer for houseplants and once or twice during winter.

PESTS AND PROBLEMS

Mealy bug and scale may affect *Fatsia*.

If plants are overwatered or temperatures are too high, the leaves turn yellow and fall. In dry air or direct summer sunlight, the leaves scorch and shrivel; move plants away from scorching sunshine. When plants are underwatered, the leaves turn pale and the margins become brown and brittle.

LONGEVITY

Fatsias eventually outgrow their space and can be planted outdoors. Mature specimens can become very large, magnificent architectural plants that enjoy a sunny or semi-shaded position in free-draining compost. The clusters of flowers are superb.

Below: Fatsia japonica *is ideal as a specimen plant, standing in a position where you can enjoy the glossy leaves. Young leaves have delicately felted undersides.*

Right: Against a plain, pale background you can appreciate the undulating leaves of x Fatshedera lizei *'Pia'. Plant three to a pot for a dense display.*

Below: Although x Fatshedera lizei *'Variegata' is slightly less vigorous than the green-leaved types, its yellow colouring is a pleasing feature.*

OTHER VARIETIES OF INTEREST

Fatsia japonica 'Variegata': Lobe tips are cream-edged.

RELATIVES OF INTEREST

x *Fatshedera lizei* (tree ivy): A hybrid between *Fatsia* and *Hedera*, with lax stems that need staking or training up a trellis.

x *Fatshedera lizei* 'Annemieke' (also sold as 'Lemon and Lime' and x *F. l.* maculata): Yellow variegation.

FICUS BENJAMINA

Under favourable conditions, the elegant weeping fig, *Ficus benjamina*, becomes a small tree. Its arching branches are lined with slender twigs, decked with delicately tipped leaves and sharply pointed buds. It is an ideal houseplant and more compact than its relative the rubber plant *(Ficus elastica)* and in its green or variegated forms makes a most attractive specimen plant.

Weeping figs, particularly the variegated types that need the extra light, flourish in bright light, with some sunshine, but always protect them from scorching midday summer sun. In partial shade, plants survive rather than thrive and growth is slow; plants in dark corners soon become misshapen as they grow towards the light. Provide moderate to warm conditions and avoid fluctuations. In winter, plants will survive in a cool room, as long as they are watered carefully. Mist them regularly with tepid rainwater if your local tapwater is hard. Misting is particularly important when room temperatures rise, as dry air damages the leaves. Stand young plants on a shallow tray of pebbles half-filled with water.

When the pot becomes congested with roots, repot plants in spring into a container one size larger. When the plant is too large to repot, topdress annually by carefully removing and replacing the top 5-7.5cm of compost. Smaller plants can be repotted in peat substitute-based compost; pot larger specimens into John Innes No 2 compost with added horticultural grit or pea gravel to give them more stability. A common problem - loss of leaves in winter - is due to the combined effects of low light levels and hot dry air from heating systems. Keep plants at moderate temperatures, move them close to a window, turn them regularly to take advantage of the extra light and mist them often. Your plant is certain to shed some leaves, but new ones will appear in spring.

1

2

3

PROPAGATION

In early summer, take healthy 7.5-10cm-long side shoots from the current season's growth as propagation material.

1 *Trim with a sharp knife just below the leaf joint and remove the basal leaves.*

2 *Insert the cutting into a 9cm pot of moist cutting compost. There is no need to dip it in hormone rooting powder; the cutting will stop 'bleeding' in contact with the compost. Firm the compost gently.*

3 *Place the pot in a loosely knotted plastic bag and put it in a warm spot away from direct light. Once roots are formed, remove the bag, acclimatize the cutting for about a week and pot it on.*

FEEDING AND WATERING

When plants are actively growing, keep the compost moist using tepid water and allow the surface to dry out between waterings. In winter or at lower temperatures keep the compost slightly moist. From spring to autumn, feed every two weeks with a general liquid houseplant fertilizer. Feed monthly during the winter.

PESTS AND PROBLEMS

Mealy bug, scale and red spider mite may affect weeping figs and other members of the *Ficus* family.

The lower leaves of weeping figs naturally turn yellow and drop with age, so that after a few years plants become bare at the base. Yellowing leaf margins and loss of older leaves at the base is usually caused by under-feeding. Direct sunshine, hot, dry air and dry compost are usually the cause of dry, shrivelled leaves; move the plant, mist it regularly and water well.

LONGEVITY

Weeping figs can last for many years and older plants become very large.

Right: *The stems of* Ficus benjamina *can be woven or twisted with extraordinary results. An advantage of this is that a plant maintained in this way does not need the support of a bamboo cane.*

Above: Ficus benjamina *'Exotica Monique' has remarkable wavy leaves with long tapering tips. A plant well-clothed with foliage creates an almost shimmering effect.*

Left: Ficus benjamina *'De Gantel' is a handsome pyramid-shaped plant with masses of leaves that create a real feeling of movement. Like all weeping figs, it is a splendid specimen plant.*

Right: *The leaves of* Ficus benjamina *'Golden King', have narrow, irregular creamy margins, initially lime green.*

FICUS ELASTICA

For years the rubber plant has been a popular houseplant and there are some wonderful variegated forms. It creates an immediate impact with its large, glossy leaves, but once established in good growing conditions, plants will rapidly outgrow their allotted space. However, they will regenerate if pruned and replacement plants are easy to propagate by tip cuttings.

PROPAGATION

Take tip cuttings about 2.5cm long, with one large leaf above the bud at the tip. Roll the leaf (underside inside) into a tube, secure it with a rubber band and support it with a cane. Keep the pot in a warm bright position inside a plastic bag. When the bud begins to grow, remove the bag and allow the plant to acclimatize. Repot when the compost is congested with roots. Alternatively, try air layering as shown here.

1 *Make an upward-slanting cut about 15-30cm from a shoot tip, two-thirds through the stem and just below the lowest leaf joint.*
2 *Use a matchstick to keep the cut surfaces open.*
3 *Coat the cut surfaces with hormone rooting powder.*
4 *Tie a piece of clear plastic to the stem below the cut and fill the tube with moist peat-substitute compost or sphagnum moss.*
5 *Tie the top of the tube against the stem and put the plant in a bright place. After about six to eight weeks roots will develop in the compost. Sever the stem below the tube.*
6 *Remove the plastic and pot up the rooted top section.*

Ficus elastica enjoy the same growing conditions as *Ficus benjamina* and once they have outgrown their allotted space can be pruned back. This can sometimes make the problem worse, however, as pruning encourages the production of side shoots. The other option is to repropagate the plant. Large plants should be grown in John Innes No 2 compost with added horticultural grit or pea gravel, which provides added weight and greater stability. Sponge the leaves occasionally with tepid water to remove accumulated dust, supporting them with your hand.

FEEDING AND WATERING

When plants are actively growing, keep the compost moist using tepid water and allow the surface to dry out between waterings.

PESTS AND PROBLEMS

Leaf loss from rubber plants is often due to overwatering.

LONGEVITY

Rubber plants will live for many years in the home.

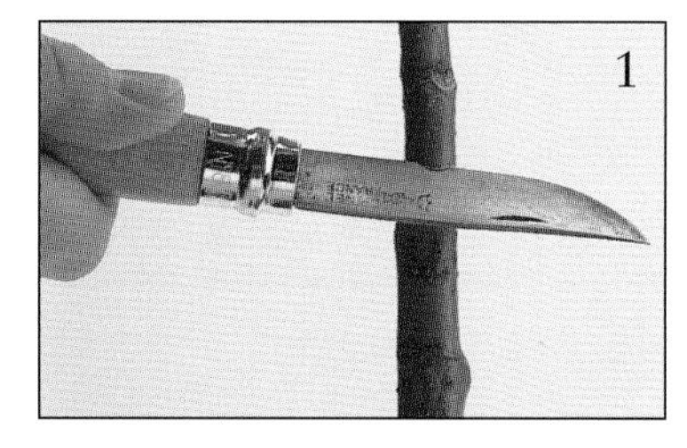

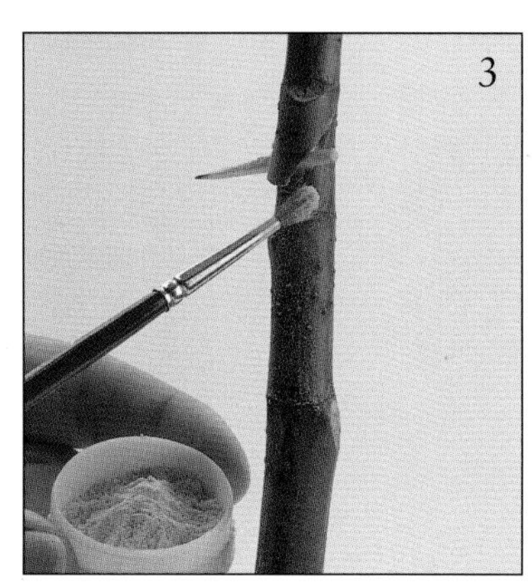

4

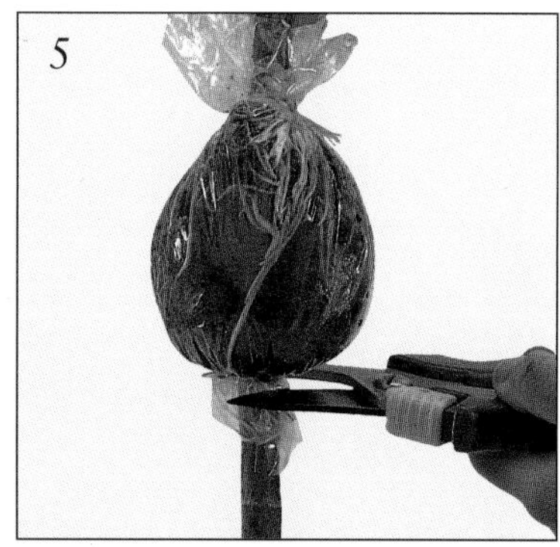

Below: There are many attractive forms of the rubber plant. This one, Ficus elastica *'Tineke', has dark- and grey-green variegations, while the younger leaves have deep burgundy leaf stems and midribs. This is a really handsome plant.*

Above: Ficus elastica *'Robusta' has broad, dark green leaves that contrast beautifully with the deep burgundy leaf sheaths.*

Above: Ficus lyrata *'Audrey' is a wonderful form of the fiddle-leaf fig. It has prominent veins and undulating leaf margins.*

Right: Ficus pumila *'Sonny' is a pretty little member of the* Ficus *family of plants that will climb or trail over the side of a pot. The heart-shaped leaves have undulating edges and irregular, creamy-white margins.*

FITTONIA

These low-growing, creeping plants from the rainforests of South America are neat and compact, which makes them ideal for bathroom shelves or bottle gardens. When several are planted together in a shallow pot they make a very attractive display, with their deep green leaves, intricately patterned with coloured veins. In good growing conditions, the plants produce spikes of yellow-green flowers.

PROPAGATION

In spring, take healthy 5-8cm-long shoot tips from the current season's growth.

1 *Trim with a sharp knife just below the leaf joint and remove the basal leaves. Using a pencil or thin cane, make four holes a few centimetres deep in a 9cm pot of moist cutting compost.*
2 *Dip the base of the cuttings in hormone rooting powder, gently tapping off the excess. Insert the cuttings and firm the compost gently around the stem.*
3 *Place the pot in a loosely knotted plastic bag, supported by four canes. Put it in a warm spot in bright but not direct light. Once roots are formed and the cuttings begin to grow, remove the bag, acclimatize the cuttings for a week and pot into separate containers.*

1

Constant warmth, high humidity and good light are the mosaic plant's chief requirements. Give it light shade in summer, but in winter, where light levels are low, move it to a bright position near a window. Provide warm to moderate, draught-free conditions and mist plants as often as possible, preferably with soft tepid water. Alternatively, stand them on a tray of pebbles filled with water to just below the base of the pot or group several plants together. Ideally, fittonias should be grown in a bottle garden, terrarium or a warm bathroom to keep them happy. They are shallow-rooted and rarely require repotting. When they are potbound, repot them in spring into half pots or shallow pans of peat substitute-based compost. Pinch out the growth points to encourage side shoots to develop and trim back creeping stems to encourage new growth.

3

2

FEEDING AND WATERING

When plants are growing, keep the compost moist with tepid water and allow it to dry out slightly between waterings. Do not overwater or allow the plants to dry out. In cooler conditions, keep the compost slightly moist. When the plant is actively growing, feed it every two weeks with a general liquid houseplant fertilizer. Feed only two or three times with a dilute solution during the winter.

PESTS AND PROBLEMS

Fittonias are generally free of pests and diseases.

In dry air or if plants are positioned in direct sunlight or underwatered, the leaves become brittle, dull and shrivel. In cold conditions or in draughts, the leaves fall.

Fittonias are particularly prone to overwatering; the leaves become yellow, and brown patches appear before the leaves fall.

LONGEVITY

After a few years, plants become straggly and should be repropagated.

Below: Fittonia verschaffeltii var. argyroneura *'Superba' has large leaves and ivory white veining. Not the easiest plant to grow, but well worth trying.*

Below: Fittonia verschaffeltii var. argyroneura *'Minima' has a mass of smaller leaves that make a neat and compact display.*

Above: F. v. var. pearcei *'Superba Red' has dark green, pink-veined leaves. The variety* F. v. var. pearcei *has leaf veins of an even brighter pink.*

Above: Fittonia verschaffeltii var. argyroneura *'Nana', a dense, compact plant with intricately veined leaves, is the least demanding of the fittonias.*

GARDENIA

Clothed in handsome foliage of rich, glossy green and adorned in double, white, waxy blooms maturing to a delicate butter yellow, the glorious gardenia exudes a refined elegance. Like many aristocrats, it also sports an exquisite, heady perfume and is particular about its lifestyle, but if you can cater for its requirements, the reward is unsurpassed.

To grow gardenias successfully, use compost for acid-loving (ericaceous) plants and mist and water them with tepid rainwater. Bear in mind that draughts, sudden temperature fluctuations, drying out of the compost and moving plants when the buds are formed all cause bud drop. Gardenias need constant moderate to warm conditions to flower, but with careful watering, will tolerate cooler conditions in winter.

Bright light throughout the year is essential, but avoid direct sunlight and lightly shade plants from mid-spring until early autumn. Pots of well-established plants can be buried in ericaceous compost or acidic soil in a sheltered sunny position outdoors from early summer to early autumn. Those that remain indoors should be well-ventilated in summer. High humidity is essential when the flower buds are forming and under warm conditions, so mist plants daily or stand them on a shallow tray of pebbles half-filled with water. This latter method is preferable when plants are in bloom, as wetting the flowers causes discoloration.

Gardenias flower better when slightly potbound, so do not repot them until the roots have almost filled the pot and are appearing through the drainage holes. When they have reached this stage and just as they start into growth in spring, repot them into a container one size larger, using ericaceous compost. Try to disturb the rootball as little as possible.

As older plants become spindly, prune them in spring by cutting back older stems by a half or two-thirds to encourage healthy new growth.

PROPAGATION

In spring, take a healthy 7.5cm-long shoot tip from the current season's growth. Trim it with a sharp knife just below a leaf joint and remove the basal leaves. Using a pencil or thin cane, make a hole a few centimetres deep in a 9cm pot of moist cutting compost for acid-loving (ericaceous) plants.

Dip the base of the cutting in hormone rooting powder, gently tapping off the excess. Insert the cutting in the compost and gently firm it around the stem. Place the pot in a loosely knotted plastic bag, supported by four canes, and put it in a warm position in indirect light.

Once roots have formed - after four to six weeks - and the cutting begins to grow, remove the bag and allow it to acclimatize for about a week.

In late summer, move the developing plant into a pot one size larger containing ericaceous compost, water moderately and feed every four weeks. Then treat it as a mature plant, potting on as required and pinching out the shoot tips to encourage bushy growth.

Left: Cuttings of this size need a pot to themselves to thrive.

FEEDING AND WATERING

Using tepid rainwater, keep the compost constantly moist but not waterlogged. In winter, at lower temperatures, allow the surface of the compost to dry out between waterings.

Apply a liquid feed for ericaceous plants or sequestered iron at the recommended strength every two weeks in summer and once or twice during winter. If hard water is your only option, use the same fertilizers every time the plant is watered, but at half strength.

PESTS AND PROBLEMS

Red spider mite and aphids may cause problems.

Bud and leaf drop are caused by underwatering and high or fluctuating temperatures. Underfeeding cold roots or hard water may cause yellowing of the leaves.

Maintain constant moderate temperatures to encourage buds to form.

LONGEVITY

With care and given good growing conditions, gardenias will give you pleasure for many years.

Above: Gardenia augusta. *A healthy plant with its luxuriant dark glossy leaves and pure white flowers is a majestic sight.*

Below: At close quarters, you can really appreciate the delicate flowers, unfurling buds and exquisite fragrance.

Below: Under good growing conditions, Gardenia augusta *will flourish and slowly develop from a small pot plant into a glorious, tall, bushy specimen plant. Remove dead flowers throughout the growing season to encourage new buds to form.*

BRINGING YOUR PLANT HOME

As they are expensive plants, protect gardenias from cold and draughts during the journey home and take care not to knock any buds off.

HEDERA

There is a multitude of shapes and colourful variegations to be found in the handsome, glossy, lobed leaves of these robust vigorous plants. Thriving in sun or shade, tolerating draughts and suitable for overwintering in an unheated room, their only apparent weakness is exposed in higher temperatures, when dry air increases their vulnerability to attack by red spider mite.

Hederas prefer bright light all year, away from scorching sunshine. They tolerate partial shade, but where light levels are low, plants become spindly and produce fewer leaves. They enjoy moderate conditions, tolerating a wide range of temperatures, but dislike fluctuations and prefer a cool rest period in winter. High temperatures at any time of year must be accompanied by increased humidity to reduce the risk of attack from red spider mite. Mist plants occasionally or stand them on a shallow tray of pebbles half-filled with water. Every two years in spring or when roots appear through the drainage holes, repot hederas into a container one size larger, using John Innes No 2 compost, and water thoroughly with tepid water. When they are in a pot of the largest convenient size, topdress annually by replacing the top 5-7.5cm of compost. Train the stems up canes, trellis or moss poles and shorten excessively long ones during the summer.

PROPAGATION

Remove stems occasionally to promote bushiness; you can use the tips as cuttings. In summer, take 7.5-12.5cm-long cuttings from the shoot tip.

1. *Trim with a sharp knife just below a leaf joint and remove the basal leaves.*
2. *Using a pencil or thin cane, make four holes a few centimetres deep in a 9cm pot of moist cutting compost. Dip the base of the cutting in hormone rooting powder, tap off the excess and insert the cutting in the compost. Firm gently around the stem.*
3. *Place the pot in a loosely knotted plastic bag supported by canes and put it in a warm spot away from direct light. Once roots are formed and the cuttings begin to grow, remove the bag, allow them to acclimatize for about a week and pot into larger containers.*

Tip cuttings can be rooted in water at room temperature in two to three weeks. Take care when potting up your cuttings because the delicate, water-filled roots are easily damaged. Do not firm the compost too vigorously around the cuttings.

FEEDING AND WATERING

When the plant is actively growing, keep the compost moist, but allow the surface to dry out between waterings. Water sparingly in winter, particularly in lower temperatures, but never let the compost dry out completely. Feed with a general liquid houseplant fertilizer every two weeks in summer and once or twice during the winter.

PESTS AND PROBLEMS

Browning leaf margins and bare spindly growth are often caused by high temperatures. Remove affected stems and move the plant to a cooler position. If light levels are too low the plant produces smaller leaves, and variegated plants will revert to green.

Ivy leaf spot appears as grey blotches on the leaves. Remove any affected leaves and spray the plant with an organic fungicide.

Aphids can be a problem.

LONGEVITY

With proper care and regular pruning, ivies can live for many years as houseplants.

Left: H. canariensis *'Montgomery' has bronze-purple stems supporting mid-green leaves that darken as they mature and have sharply angled lobes.*

Above: The leaves of the magnificent H. algeriensis *'Gloire de Marengo' are variegated with patches of light green, silvery grey and yellow.*

OTHER VARIETIES OF INTEREST

H. helix 'Chicago': Red-green stems with slightly lobed, pale green leaves.
H. h. 'Glacier': Leaves are grey-green with silver-grey blotches and thin cream margins.
H. helix 'Kolibri': Dark green leaves with bold white splashes and spots.
H. h. 'Luzii': Leaves are pale grey-green, mottled and spotted with yellow-green.

HIBISCUS

Giant hibiscus blooms, vibrant, yet delicate as tissue paper, are the dazzling highlight of many gardens in warm climates. The flowers of fleeting beauty are produced in constant succession. Gardeners in cooler climates may not be able to grow them outdoors, but as houseplants, given bright light and warmth, they will certainly bloom in profusion for many years.

1

2

3

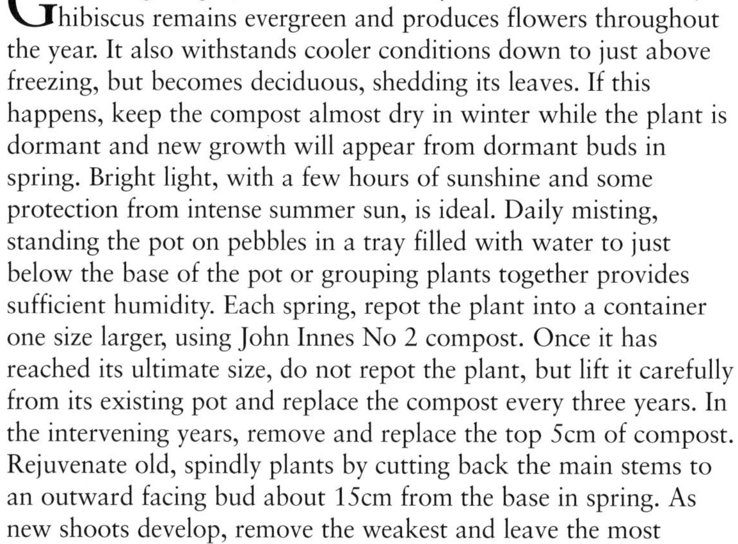

Given bright light, moderate humidity and constant warmth, hibiscus remains evergreen and produces flowers throughout the year. It also withstands cooler conditions down to just above freezing, but becomes deciduous, shedding its leaves. If this happens, keep the compost almost dry in winter while the plant is dormant and new growth will appear from dormant buds in spring. Bright light, with a few hours of sunshine and some protection from intense summer sun, is ideal. Daily misting, standing the pot on pebbles in a tray filled with water to just below the base of the pot or grouping plants together provides sufficient humidity. Each spring, repot the plant into a container one size larger, using John Innes No 2 compost. Once it has reached its ultimate size, do not repot the plant, but lift it carefully from its existing pot and replace the compost every three years. In the intervening years, remove and replace the top 5cm of compost. Rejuvenate old, spindly plants by cutting back the main stems to an outward facing bud about 15cm from the base in spring. As new shoots develop, remove the weakest and leave the most

PROPAGATION

Visitors are certain to ask for cuttings. Fortunately, *Hibiscus* roots easily and you should have plenty to spare.

1 *Take a healthy shoot tip about 7.5-10cm long from the current season's growth. Trim it with a sharp knife just below a leaf joint and remove the basal leaves.*

2 *Use a pencil or thin cane to make a hole a few centimetres deep in a 9cm pot of moist cutting mixture. Dip the base of the cutting in hormone rooting powder, tap off the excess and insert the cutting. Firm the compost gently around the stem.*

3 *Place the pot in a loosely knotted plastic bag supported by four canes and put it in a warm corner away from direct light. Once roots form and the cutting begins to grow, remove the bag and allow the cutting to acclimatize for about a week before moving it onto display. Remember to pinch out the growing tips of the cuttings you take to encourage bushy growth and repot them into larger containers when the compost starts to become congested with roots.*

FEEDING AND WATERING

If conditions remain warm all year, keep compost moist, but allow the surface to dry out slightly between waterings. Avoid water-logging. Feed actively growing plants every two weeks from spring to autumn with a flowering houseplant fertilizer. In the years when plants are cut back, feed them initially with foliage houseplant fertilizer to encourage healthy new stems, and then with flowering houseplant fertilizer.

PESTS AND PROBLEMS

Aphids and whitefly may cause problems. Look out for red spider mite.

Bud drop often occurs with newly acquired plants due to the shock of environmental change, but it can also result from underwatering, under-feeding and fluctuating or sudden temperature changes. Dry air causes curling leaves; mist the plant with a fine spray. Leaves may drop due to under- or overwatering and draughts, but this also occurs naturally in low winter temperatures. A shortage of flower buds is usually due to lack of sunlight or fertilizer or using the wrong fertilizer.

OTHER VARIETIES OF INTEREST

H. schizopetalus: Delicate hanging flowers with fringed petals. The stems are weak and better trained over arches.
H. rosa-sinensis 'Cooperi': Pink-and-white variegated leaves and red flowers.
H. r.-s. 'Helene': Glossy green leaves and rose-pink flowers.
H. r.-s. 'Natal': Large white flowers and a red central blotch.
H. r.-s. 'Rio': Blush-pink flowers with crimson central splash.

Right: Hibiscus rosa-sinensis *'Paramaribo' produces delicately veined crimson blooms against a background of dark green, deeply veined leaves.*

Left: *Less flamboyant than its extrovert relatives,* H. rosa-sinensis *'Casablanca' projects its white flowers upwards so that you can enjoy their beauty.*

Above: *The apricot and crimson flowers of* Hibiscus rosa-sinensis *'Bangkok' will bring a touch of the exotic orient into your home.*

HOYA

From late spring to early autumn, hanging clusters of sweetly fragrant, star-shaped flowers emerge among the twining stems and succulent leaves of this stunning houseplant. They are at their most fragrant at night and produce copious amounts of nectar. This exotic tropical treasure is surprisingly hardy, tolerating winter temperatures almost down to freezing. Water with care.

PROPAGATION

Take 7.5-10cm-long shoot tip cuttings in early summer.

1 *Trim with a sharp knife just below a leaf joint and remove the basal leaves. Dip the cut ends in hormone rooting powder. Using a pencil or thin cane, make 2-3 holes a few centimetres deep in a 9cm pot of moist cutting compost.*

2 *Dip the base of each cutting in hormone rooting powder, gently tapping off the excess. Insert the cuttings and firm the compost gently around the stem. Place the pot in a loosely knotted plastic bag supported by four canes and put it in a warm position away from direct light. Once roots have formed after about two months and the cuttings begin to grow, remove the bag and water sparingly, allowing them to acclimatize for about a week. Then as they establish, start regular feeding and repot as necessary, pinching out growth tips to encourage branching.*

Wax plants need bright light to flourish, particularly during the winter when light levels are low, but protect them from scorching summer sun. In poor light, flower buds drop and growth is spindly. If the light is very low and no flowers form, move plants to a brighter position and remember to feed them regularly with a fertilizer for flowering houseplants. Hoyas flower better when slightly potbound. They dislike draughts and prefer constant warm conditions in the growing season and a cool winter rest with careful watering. *Hoya carnosa* tolerates lower temperatures than other types. Provide constant humidity in the growing season by misting or standing plants on a tray of pebbles half-filled with water. High humidity is not necessary in cool winter conditions. If the compost becomes heavily congested with roots, repot plants into a container one size larger in late spring, using a peat substitute-based compost with added sharp sand or perlite to improve drainage and to allow air to reach the roots.

Do not move plants once the flower buds appear. When you remove spent blooms and their stalks, leave the flowering spurs, as these will produce flowers in future years. After flowering, shorten any long growths that spoil the shape of the plant. When you buy a wax plant, the stems are usually trained around wire hoops. As the plant matures, you can train it up trellising, moss poles or a tripod of canes, or grow it in a hanging basket as a trailing plant.

FEEDING AND WATERING

As these plants are shallow-rooted, take particular care to avoid overwatering and prevent drying out. Use tepid water to keep the compost moist when plants are actively growing, rewatering when the surface begins to dry out. In cooler winter temperatures, water sparingly to keep the compost just moist, but do not let it dry out completely. Feed every two weeks with a liquid fertilizer for flowering houseplants and once or twice in winter if the plant is kept in warmer conditions.

PESTS AND PROBLEMS

Wax plants are generally trouble-free, but mealy bug may cause a problem.

Excessively low temperatures and over- or underwatering causes leaves to yellow, wither and fall. If leaves become dry, curl up and turn pale, the problem is excess sunshine or low temperatures. Remove any affected leaves and move the plant to a more favourable position.

LONGEVITY

A well-cared-for plant will last for many years.

Left: Hoya lanceolata *ssp.* bella *produces masses of stems clothed in glossy green leaves and decorated with clusters of waxy starlike flowers. A well-grown specimen in full flower is a glorious houseplant.*

Above: *The exquisite flowers of* Hoya lanceolata *ssp.* bella *hanging from the trailing stems have a wonderful fragrance.*

Left: *Train the stems of* Hoya multiflora *up a cane or trellis. The arching flowers drip nectar, so protect the surface below.*

Right: *Some hoyas, such as this* Hoya carnosa *'Tricolor', have variegated foliage that provides interest all year round.*

HYDRANGEA

This is one of the few hardy plants from cool temperate zones that has become a popular houseplant. Bought as a temporary floral display, hydrangeas are usually discarded after flowering, but you can plant them outdoors in a flower border or container and they will last for many years. The compact, globular clusters of blue, pink or white florets will flourish in a cool bright room.

Hydrangeas need a bright, cool position, as the life expectancy of the flowers, which can last upwards of six weeks, is considerably reduced in warm conditions. To maintain humidity, mist plants occasionally or stand them on a shallow tray of pebbles filled with water to just below the base of the pot. Once plants have finished flowering, do not dispose of them or shred them for the compost heap. Instead, cut back the main stems by half, wait until there is no danger of frost before planting the hydrangea outdoors and watering thoroughly. The reason for waiting is that although hydrangeas are 'hardy', your plant, having spent several weeks indoors and become used to protected conditions, will be less frost-tolerant and needs time to acclimatize to the weather outside.

When planting hydrangeas outdoors, remember that pink varieties turn blue in ericaceous compost or acid soil and blue varieties turn pink in alkaline soil. Be sure to plant hydrangeas outdoors at the level of the compost in the pot, no deeper.

1

2

3

PROPAGATION

Take cuttings from healthy shoots in mid- to late summer from the ripening wood of the current year's growth.

1 *Trim each 7.5-10cm-long shoot tip just below a leaf joint. Remove basal leaves.*
2 *Dip the base of the cuttings in hormone rooting powder, tap off the excess, insert into moist compost and firm in.*
3 *Place the pot in a loosely knotted plastic bag and put it in a warm spot away from direct light. Once the cuttings begin to grow, remove the bag to acclimatize them and pot on as necessary into containers of ericaceous compost or John Innes No 2.*

FEEDING AND WATERING

Water hydrangeas regularly, keeping the compost moist at all times. If plants are allowed to dry out they soon collapse and the flowers quickly fade. Use rainwater or soft water if your hydrangeas are blue, but hard water is fine for pink hydrangeas. Feed hydrangeas every two weeks; those with pink flowers should have a general liquid houseplant fertilizer. If the flowers are blue, feed them with a general liquid fertilizer for ericaceous (acid-loving) plants if you wish to retain the colour.

PESTS AND PROBLEMS

Red spider mite may be troublesome indoors.

LONGEVITY

Once planted outdoors, hydrangeas are long lived.

***Left:** The mauve-blue florets encircle the dense flower clusters and developing buds of this striking* Hydrangea macrophylla *'Teller's Blue'.*

***Right:** The snow-white florets cluster like confetti around the pale blue flowers and violet buds of this* Hydrangea macrophylla *'Libelle', once known as 'Teller's White'.*

***Left:** The massed flower heads on this specimen of* Hydrangea macrophylla *'Bodensee' create an instant impact.*

***Below:** The young green mopheads soon become a bright, rich pink. Choose a colour to match the decor of your room.*

HYPOESTES

This compact, pretty little plant from the tropical rainforests of Madagascar is grown for its colourful foliage. The dark green leaves are marked with spots from pink through to white, often merging to form patches that look like splashes of paint. Enjoying warmth and humidity, they grow well in a terrarium or on a brightly lit windowsill, where their vivid colours can be fully enjoyed.

To keep their variegation prominent, polkadot plants need bright light with some sunshine, but not scorching summer sun. If light levels are too low, growth slows, the vivid coloration gradually fades and the leaves turn green. Temperatures should be moderate throughout the year and the plants also enjoy constant humidity. Spray them frequently each day with tepid water - more often in hot dry conditions - or place them on pebbles in a tray filled with water to just below the base of the pot. As with many houseplants, polkadot plants dislike cool draughts.

When the pot becomes congested with roots, repot the plant into a container one size larger. Do this in spring, using a peat-substitute potting mixture. Pinch out the tips of the young growth to encourage bushiness and also pinch out the insignificant mauve flowers. Keep the leaves dust-free by wiping them carefully with a damp sponge or soft brush; make-up brushes are ideal! Cut straggly plants back to the base in spring, then feed and water them regularly to encourage new growth.

1

PROPAGATION

Take 7.5-10cm-long tip cuttings in mid-spring to summer.

1 *Trim with a sharp knife just below the leaf joint and remove the basal leaves.*

2 *Dip the base of the cuttings in hormone rooting powder and tap off the excess.*

3 *Plant the cuttings in a 7.5cm pot of moist peat-substitute based cutting compost.*

4 *Cover them with a plastic bag, keep them warm in bright, filtered light and when new growth begins, remove the plastic bag so that they can acclimatize. Increase watering. Trim back young plants so that they branch out and take cuttings regularly to keep plants young and vigorous.*

FEEDING AND WATERING

Keep the compost moist, watering liberally from spring to autumn and sparingly in winter. Allow the surface of the compost to dry out between waterings. Feed fortnightly during summer with a general houseplant fertilizer. If the plant is allowed to flower it may become dormant. When this happens, reduce watering until new growth appears.

PESTS AND PROBLEMS

Hypoestes are usually pest-free. Loss of leaves and lacklustre growth can be caused by underwatering or low temperatures. Cut back bare stems to 7.5-10cm and keep the compost moist. Move the plant to a warmer, more humid position. Strong direct sunshine and dry air cause scorching and browning of the leaf tips. Move the plant to bright light (but not direct sunlight) and increase humidity.

LONGEVITY

Older plants make attractive small bushes with slightly lax growth that, with regular trimming or pinching out, can last for several years.

OTHER VARIETIES OF INTEREST
H. p. 'Carmina': Has brighter red leaves than its relatives.

Below: *Grow* Hypoestes *individually in small pots or plant a selection of each in a shallow pan for a brightly coloured mixed display. Grouping several plants together helps to maintain humidity and increases the impact of their vivid colours. Their leaf colour is more pronounced when displayed against a pale background. Polkadot plants make neat, bushy plants if you pinch out the growth tips regularly.*

IMPATIENS

An old favourite, noted for its ease of cultivation and almost iridescent blooms. These are produced throughout the year under favourable conditions. To the many existing varieties has been added 'New Guinea Hybrids', with their richly coloured variegated leaves and masses of flowers in colours from bright scarlet to pale mauve. Together, they provide an almost bewildering choice.

Bright light, away from direct summer sun is ideal for busy Lizzies; in areas where winter light levels are low, give them as much light as possible. They prefer moderate temperatures, but tolerate cooler conditions if you water them carefully. Keep your plants well away from draughts. If temperatures increase, particularly in centrally heated rooms, make sure that you keep the surrounding air humid, as they dislike dry air. Mist plants regularly with a fine spray of tepid water, but avoid wetting the flowers, as they are easily marked; alternatively, group several plants together or stand them on a tray of pebbles filled with water to just below the base of the pot.

Busy Lizzies flower better when slightly potbound. Repot them in spring, into a pot one size larger, when roots appear through the drainage holes. Use John Innes No 2 or peat substitute-based compost. Pinch out growth tips to encourage bushiness in young plants. Prune older, spindly plants to within a few inches of the base in spring; again, pinch out the tips as the plants regrow. Stake plants if they become tall, as the brittle stems break easily.

PROPAGATION

Stem tip cuttings will root easily in compost or water.

1 *Take a non-flowering shoot about 7.5-10cm long, cut just below a leaf joint using a very sharp knife and remove the basal leaves.*
2 *Cover the top of a glass bowl or jar with aluminium foil or several layers of clingfilm, make holes in it and insert the cuttings so that at least the bottom 3cm of the stem is in the water.*
3 *Place in a bright position and pot up when roots develop.*

FEEDING AND WATERING

Keep the compost moist, allowing the surface to dry out between waterings. Reduce watering in winter and avoid waterlogging. When the plant is actively growing, feed it every two weeks with a general houseplant fertilizer. In winter, feed it once or twice.

PESTS AND PROBLEMS

Red spider mite, aphids and white fly may cause problems.

Leaves wilt if temperatures are too high or when plants are underwatered. In low temperatures or when watering is erratic, leaves become yellow and are shed.

Few flowers appear in low light, low temperatures or if plants are repotted too often. Flowers are shed in dry air or if the compost dries out. Older varieties become spindly with age, but this is encouraged by low light and high temperatures. Newer varieties are more compact.

The stems rot if plants are overwatered, particularly in cooler conditions.

LONGEVITY

With regular pruning, plants can last for several years.

Busy Lizzie

Left: *The New Guinea hybrids are a superb group of robust plants, noted for their dark and sometimes variegated foliage and the masses of brightly coloured flowers produced right through from spring to the autumn.*

Above: *The rich dark leaves, create the perfect background for the orange-red flowers. Imagine the impact of several plants grouped together!*

Left: *Every plant is full of colour; even the stems and midribs of the leaves are tinged dark red, a subtle touch enhanced by the pink flowers.*

OTHER VARIETIES OF INTEREST

Impatiens niamniamensis 'Congo Cockatoo': Dark green, paddle-shaped leaves on long stems and unusual bright yellow and red flowers growing directly from the stems.

Impatiens walleriana: Succulent stems and a naturally spindly growth habit. It bears white, red or pink flowers.

'New Guinea' hybrids: Bright, multicoloured leaves.

JASMINUM

Dense clusters of buds, which are flushed pale pink, open to reveal fragrant flowers of the purest white, displayed to perfection against a backcloth of feathery foliage and wiry twining stems. Usually bought trained round a wire hoop, this energetic climber can reach massive proportions, even with regular pruning. It is an easy and worthy substitute for the Madagascar jasmine *(Stephanotis).*

1

2

3

Good light will encourage *Jasminum polyanthum* to flower, and a position on a bright windowsill away from draughts and scorching sunshine is ideal. In the growing season, the plants need, moderate temperatures, and once there is no danger of frost, they will grow outdoors in a bright or lightly shaded position. Do remember to bring them indoors before the first autumn frosts. In winter they prefer a cool room, but tolerate temperatures almost down to freezing if carefully watered; whatever you do, keep them away from high temperatures and the drying effect of radiators.

Mist leaves occasionally with tepid water, except when the plant is in bloom, or stand the plants on shallow trays of pebbles filled with water to just below the base of the pot. Repot them in early spring into John Innes No 2 compost. When plants reach the maximum convenient pot size, carefully remove and replace the top 7.5cm of compost each spring. Immediately after flowering, untie the stems from the wire hoop, remove any weak growth and cut back older stems to within 5cm of the base. Cut back vigorous stems by one-third and the side shoots projecting from them to one or two buds. Twine the stems back round the hoop, tie them in again and tie in new growths as they appear. As older plants increase in size, train them up trellis or a tripod of bamboo canes.

PROPAGATION

From midsummer to early autumn, take tip or heel cuttings from the side shoots.

1 *Take a healthy 7.5-10cm-long shoot tip from the current season's growth and trim it with a sharp knife just below a leaf joint. Heel cuttings are the same size; take them from the side shoots, with a small piece of the main stem still attached. Trim the 'heel' with a sharp knife. In both cases, remove the basal leaves.*

2 *Dip the base in hormone rooting powder, tap off the excess and make a hole with a cane or pencil in a 7.5cm pot of moist cutting compost.*

3 *Insert four canes for support, then put the pot in a loosely knotted plastic bag and place it in a bright position. When the cuttings have rooted after four to five weeks, move them into 10cm pots of John Innes No 2. Pinch out the main growth point when the stem is 20-30cm long to encourage side shooting.*

FEEDING AND WATERING

Use tepid water and keep the compost constantly moist but not waterlogged. In winter, allow the surface to dry out between waterings. When the plant is actively growing, feed it every two weeks with a general houseplant fertilizer.

PESTS AND PROBLEMS

Aphids and mealy bug can cause problems.

When you first bring the plants home, the flower buds may turn yellow and fall off as a result of the shock of being moved; give them good light, a constant temperature and protection on the journey to your home.

In a warm dry atmosphere, direct sunshine, or if a plant is underwatered, the leaves curl, dry, shrivel and fall; move plants into a cooler room and mist the foliage if the plant is not in flower. Check the compost for underwatering.

LONGEVITY

Jasmines can be very long lived if well cared for.

Left: *When grown as a houseplant, the common white jasmine,* Jasminum officinale, *needs regular pruning to keep it under control. If its excessive vigour becomes a problem, you can always plant it outdoors.*

Above: *The leaves of* Jasminum officinale *'Argenteovariegatum' feature an extraordinary combination of colours. Many are flushed with pink.*

Below: *Throughout the flowering season,* Jasminum polyanthum *is swathed in clusters of white, starlike flowers and masses of buds.*

JUSTICIA

This small twiggy shrub, with its downy foliage, straggly growth and arching stems, is grown for its fascinating curved flower heads. Their overlapping brown-tinged, salmon-pink segments do indeed resemble the jointed body of a shrimp. Under good conditions, white flowers emerge from between these segments throughout the year. It is easy to grow and ideal for children.

Shrimp plants need bright light, moderate temperatures and humidity to thrive. Bright light is essential for the coloration of flower heads, so a position with some sunlight early or late in the day is ideal, but shade them from strong summer sun. Keep the plants in a moderate, airy position in summer, as excessive heat encourages spindly growth. They will tolerate cool winter conditions if you water them carefully. Shrimp plants require moderate humidity, so mist occasionally with tepid water or stand them on a shallow tray of pebbles filled with water to just below the base of the pot. Repot as necessary in spring when the pot becomes congested with roots, using a John Innes No 2 or peat substitute-based compost and a pot one size larger. Once the maximum convenient pot size is reached, topdress the plant annually in spring by carefully removing and replacing the top 5-7.5cm of compost. As the stems develop, pinch out the main growth tips to encourage bushiness. When the plant begins growing in spring, cut it back by half to two-thirds each year to just above a leaf joint, and remove the faded flower heads regularly to encourage continuous flowering throughout the year. Put several plants in a pot for a good display.

Propagation

In spring, use the stems you have removed during pruning as propagation material. Take healthy shoot tips about 5-7.5cm long from the current season's growth.

1 *Choose a stem with no flowers or remove the flower buds. Trim with a sharp knife just below the leaf joint and remove the basal leaves.*

2 *Using a pencil or thin cane, make several holes a few centimetres deep in a 9cm pot of moist cutting compost. Dip the base of the cuttings in hormone rooting powder, gently tapping off the excess. Insert the cuttings and firm the compost gently around the stem.*

3 *Place the pot in a loosely knotted plastic bag supported by four canes, and put it in a warm corner away from direct light. After six to eight weeks, once roots are formed and the cuttings begin to grow, remove the bag, allow the cuttings to acclimatize for about a week and then pot them into containers, three or four to a pot. When young, remove the first flowers to encourage the new plants to become established.*

Feeding and watering

Keep the compost moist, allowing the surface to dry out between waterings and water sparingly in winter, particularly in lower temperatures. Feed weekly with a half strength solution of liquid fertilizer for flowering plants when the plant is actively growing and monthly during the winter.

Pests and problems

Plants are usually free from pests and problems but can suffer from red spider mite in hot dry conditions.

Overwatering causes brown patches on the leaves. Low light levels, high temperatures or a combination of both cause spindly growth. Pale yellow bracts are caused by insufficient light. Plants shed their leaves if they become potbound or need feeding.

Longevity

Well-fed and cared-for plants last for several years.

Shrimp plant

***Below:** Looking at the segmented bracts of* Justicia brandegeeana*, it is clear to see how it became known as the shrimp plant. It is easy to grow and fun for children to try.*

Right: Justicia brandegeeana *'Yellow Queen' is a magnificent form, with bright, yellow-golden bracts that clothe the plant in glorious colour. It is worth seeking out for its flamboyant coloration and makes a welcome contrast to the shrimp plant.*

***Below:** Surprisingly,* Justicia rizzinii *is a relative of the shrimp plant, but it looks very different. The flowers are bright scarlet with a yellow tip and enliven any room from autumn to spring.*

KALANCHOE

There are many cultivars of *Kalanchoe blossfeldiana,* a vigorous, bushy succulent that is rewarding and easy to grow. Its dark green, glossy leaves are the ideal backdrop for the dense-domed clusters of vivid, long-lasting flowers. Many of its relatives look completely different, with beautiful, delicately marked leaves and unusual profiles ranging from the beautiful to the bizarre.

Kalanchoes need good light, with some morning or afternoon sun, and as much light as possible in winter. They tolerate temperatures from hot to just above freezing, but thrive in moderate to warm conditions. The foliage types need a winter rest in a cool room. One great advantage of these plants is that they tolerate dry air, which means that misting is unnecessary.

Kalanchoe blossfeldiana cultivars usually end up on the compost heap once they have finished flowering, but if you like a challenge, you can encourage them to bloom the following year. Prune the plant back to within a few centimetres of the base after flowering and place it in a shady position. Keep the compost dry for about four weeks and then return the plant to a bright position. Water and feed it as normal and then from mid-autumn, give it ten hours of daylight followed by complete darkness every day over a period of two months before returning it to a bright position.

Repot foliage kalanchoes before they become potbound, so check plants each spring and repot as necessary. Good drainage is vital, so put a 2cm layer of clay pot fragments or perlite into the bottom of the pot and use a succulent and cactus compost. After flowering, remove faded flower stalks and stake tall foliage varieties as necessary.

The trailing-stemmed kalanchoe hybrids do need occasional misting when they are in flower. Cut back older plants to within a few centimetres of the base after flowering to encourage new growth, and feed them monthly in winter.

PROPAGATION

Take a healthy, 7.5-10cm-long shoot tip from the current season's growth, shown here on *Kalanchoe pumila.*

1 *Trim with a sharp knife just below a leaf joint and remove the basal leaves.*

2 *Make several holes a few centimetres deep in a 9cm pot of moist cactus and succulent compost. Dip the base of the cuttings in hormone rooting powder, gently tapping off the excess. Insert the cuttings, firm the compost and place the pot in a warm, bright position. Once the cuttings begin to grow and have produced plenty of roots, separate them and pot them into individual containers.*

Grow flowering types of kalanchoes from seed in spring.

FEEDING AND WATERING

Although kalanchoes endure occasional drought, water plants thoroughly in summer, allowing the compost surface to dry out before rewatering. Avoid overwatering. In winter, during the rest period, keep the compost slightly moist and increase watering in spring as the plant slowly begins to grow. Feed with a half strength solution of general houseplant fertilizer every two weeks in summer, but not at all during winter.

PESTS AND PROBLEMS

Mealy bug and aphids may affect kalanchoes.

Leaves shrivel if plants are underwatered and rot if they are overwatered.

LONGEVITY

Flowering kalanchoes can be replaced annually and are only worth retaining for two seasons at the most. Others will last for many years.

1

2

Right: *Kalanchoe 'Tessa' is a trailing type that produces clusters of hanging, bell-shaped pale orange flowers. It is ideal for a hanging basket display.*

Left: *The bright yellow flowers of this* Kalanchoe blossfeldiana *provide a pleasing alternative to the many red and pink cultivars.*

Right: *The grey-green leaves with a white 'bloom' are the perfect background for the carmine-pink flowers of* Kalanchoe pumila.

OTHER VARIETIES OF INTEREST

Kalanchoe 'Wendy': One of the trailing types. It has rose-pink flowers. The mouth of the flower tube is cream.

Foliage types:

Kalanchoe diagremontianum 'Devils Backbone': Purple-blotched leaves. Tiny plantlets produced at the margins root easily.

Kalanchoe tubiflora 'Chandelier Plant': Tubular, blotched grey-green leaves. Plantlets are produced at the leaf tips and root easily.

MARANTA

Ornately marked leaves are the eye-catching feature of this treasure from the South American rainforest; equally fascinating is the way the leaves fold together at night to prevent water loss, giving maranta the alternative common name of prayer plants. Its pale green leaves with a satin sheen are marked with dark green blotches and several varieties are delicately veined.

Marantas require moderate light throughout the year, and should be shaded from bright light or direct sunshine, which scorches or bleaches the leaves. In areas where winter light levels are low, they need as much light as possible. Constant moderate temperatures encourage good growth, although cool conditions are tolerated in winter with reduced watering. Marantas need high humidity, so group plants together, spray them regularly with tepid water or stand them on a shallow tray of pebbles filled with water to just below the base of the pot. Avoid siting plants near radiators or other places where they are affected by dry air. Because they enjoy low to moderate light levels and high humidity, they are perfect plants for bottle gardens or the bathroom. As the compost becomes congested with roots, about every two years, repot marantas in spring into pots one size larger, using a peat substitute-based compost; as they have shallow root systems, shallow pans or half pots are ideal. To keep your plant looking neat and tidy, remove any straggly growths that spoil its shape.

1

PROPAGATION

You can divide marantas in spring when growth becomes congested and the plants need repotting.

1 *Carefully remove a mature plant from the pot and prise it into smaller sections. Make sure each section has a healthy set of roots.*

2 *Repot the sections into a peat substitute-based compost. After repotting, soak the compost thoroughly using tepid water and allow the surface to dry out before rewatering. Place the pot inside a loosely knotted plastic bag until the plant is established and new growth appears. Pot on as necessary, ideally into shallow pans.*

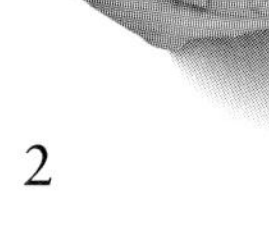

2

FEEDING AND WATERING

During the growing season, keep the compost moist but beware of overwatering. When the plant is actively growing, feed it every two weeks with a liquid fertilizer for foliage houseplants. In winter, particularly in cool conditions, allow the compost surface to dry out between waterings and feed occasionally.

PESTS AND PROBLEMS

Marantas are usually trouble-free but may suffer from red spider mite in dry air.

Direct sunshine and dry air cause browning of the leaf tips and margins. Increase humidity and move the plant to a better position.

LONGEVITY

Under good growing conditions, marantas can live for many years.

Left: *With a little imagination you can see why the leaf markings on* Maranta leuconeura *var.* kerchoveana *give this plant the common names of rabbit's tracks or rabbit's foot plant. The undersides of the leaves are pale blue-grey.*

Below: *The young leaves of* Maranta leuconeura *var.* erythroneura *unfurl to display their particularly attractive markings and coloration.*

Above: Maranta bicolor *has rich green leaves with dark markings and purple undersides. Note the tiny white flowers with purple blotches.*

An alternative method of propagation

In late spring or summer, take tip cuttings with two or three leaves from new shoots at the base of the plant. They take about six weeks to root in water. When the roots appear, plant three cuttings into a 7.5cm pot of peat substitute-based cutting compost. Pot them on as required.

MONSTERA

As a houseplant, this giant evergreen climber, with its deep green glossy leaves, angled, perforated and notched like a modern sculpture, shows much of the exuberance that takes it high into the trees of its natural rainforest habitat, clinging to its hosts with long aerial roots. In good conditions, white flowers are followed by edible pineapple-flavoured fruits; a delicious monster indeed!

Swiss cheese plants prefer bright filtered light or partial shade, but can be placed in direct sunlight when the sun is weaker in the winter. If there is too much sunlight, the leaves become pale and bleached with yellow patches and if there is too little, the plants respond by producing small or juvenile leaves or simply stop growing. Average room temperatures are adequate for healthy growth and these plants appreciate good humidity, so regular misting with tepid water, particularly when they are growing actively, is essential; young plants can stand on a tray of pebbles filled with water to just below the base of the pot.

Repot plants each year in spring using a peat substitute-based compost, or John Innes No 2 to give larger plants stability. Once the final pot size is reached - probably a 25-30cm pot - topdress the plant each year by removing and replacing the top 5-7.5cm of compost and repotting into the same pot every three years. Large pots will be heavy and may be difficult to move. If plants outgrow their allotted space, prune them back in spring to just above a leaf joint on the stem; they will regrow.

Train as many aerial roots as possible around a moss pole or into the compost and remove the remainder with sharp secateurs. If there is space, train plants around the room using twine, wires or trellis. Gently sponge the leaves with a soft, damp cloth to remove dust.

1

2

PROPAGATION

Propagate *Monstera* by taking cuttings in early spring.

1 *Remove a stem section with one or two mature leaves and insert it in a 10cm pot of moist cutting compost or equal parts of peat-substitute compost and sharp sand.*

2 *Enclose the cutting in a plastic bag and keep it warm in bright, filtered light. If the leaf is too large, roll it into a tube with the underside on the inside and secure it with a rubber band. The cutting will root in warm conditions. When new growth appears, repot the cutting and treat it as a mature plant. If you want several cuttings, remove a good length of material from the top of a stem and cut it into joints about 7.5cm long, each with a single leaf, and care for them in a similar manner.*

FEEDING AND WATERING

When the plant is actively growing, water it thoroughly, allowing the compost surface to dry out slightly between waterings. Water sparingly in winter, so that the compost is only slightly moist and allow the top third to dry out before watering again. Feed with a general houseplant fertilizer every 10-14 days in summer and autumn, but only once or twice in winter.

PESTS AND PROBLEMS

Brown or yellow patches on the leaves and rotting roots are usually caused by over-watering. Another sign is water droplets on the leaf margins, particularly early in the day, as if the plant was 'crying'. Allow the compost to dry out and increase the interval between waterings.

If the stems rot in winter, the plant is overwatered and temperatures are too low. Repot and keep the compost warm and almost dry.

LONGEVITY

Swiss cheese plants can become very large specimens, thriving indoors for many years. Pots with large plants can be difficult to move.

Below: Monstera deliciosa *is an extremely popular foliage houseplant. The bright green, glossy young leaves are especially attractive.*

Above: It is worth seeking out the wonderful M. deliciosa *'Variegata', whose leaves are boldly marked with splashes and patches of creamy white.*

Right: Monstera obliqua *has highly perforated, bright green leaves, which give the plant an unusual 'shredded' appearance. It grows well up a moss pole.*

NOLINA

The deserts of Southeastern Mexico are home to this weird and wonderful houseplant. It has a swollen scaly base that is used for storing water and straplike, arching leaves erupt from the top of its narrow stem in a haphazard manner. It is very slow-growing; starting life displayed on a table it may, many years later, become a large specimen plant in the corner of a room.

To grow well, *Nolina* (formerly known as *Beaucarnea)* needs good, bright light and sunshine throughout the year; in lower light levels growth is almost non-existent. *Nolina* is the ideal plant for a position in fluctuating temperatures, which many houseplants would find too hostile; moderate temperatures are ideal, but *Nolina* is quite happy in summer warmth and tolerates cool winter conditions if the compost remains dry. Coming from the desert, this plant likes dry air and a well-ventilated position. It will thrive outdoors in summer, providing it is protected from heavy downpours.

Repot *Nolina* in spring when it has outgrown its current accommodation. Use a mixture of John Innes No 2 with added grit or sharp sand, or a peat substitute-based compost with added sharp sand or perlite.

The leaf tips naturally become brown with age and can be removed without damaging the plant. Position the plant carefully and take care when handling the leaves or standing near the plant. If you catch the leaves at the wrong angle, they can quite easily cut you.

***Right:** Plants sometimes send out short side shoots near the base, but these do not grow very large. Offsets, which also appear at the base, can be detached and used as propagation material.*

PROPAGATION

Nolina sometimes produces offsets; detach these carefully at repotting time and pot them in the same mixture as used for adult plants. Moisten the compost and stand the plant in a warm bright position until it becomes established.

FEEDING AND WATERING

In summer, water regularly with tepid water, allowing the compost surface to dry out between waterings. Water occasionally in winter, allowing the compost to dry out completely before rewatering. Judge this by pushing your finger into the compost or use a moisture meter. From spring to autumn, feed plants monthly with a liquid fertilizer for succulents and cacti.

PESTS AND PROBLEMS

Red spider mite may affect *Nolina*. In poor light, the leaves become pale and limp; they need bright light to flourish. A weak plant lacking in vigour is usually a sign of underfeeding. The lower leaves naturally fall as the plant matures, leaving just a tuft of leaves at the top of the stem.

LONGEVITY

These slow-growing plants can last for very many years.

Left: *This older specimen of* Nolina *has several growth points and is like a miniature tree. The leaves resemble a tangled mass of green ribbons. It takes several years for them to reach a decent size, but it is well worth the wait.*

Below: *A young plant, showing the swollen base and arching leaves. It is ideal as a specimen plant, particularly in a room with modern decor, where it resembles a living sculpture.*

PELARGONIUM

Pelargoniums are among the most popular houseplants and there are hundreds of these spectacular succulents to choose from. They display an extraordinary range of flower colour, foliage form, variegation and growth habit; some even have aromatic foliage. Easy to propagate and simple to grow, pelargoniums will flower almost constantly throughout the year in favourable conditions.

PROPAGATION

In late summer, take a healthy shoot tip 7.5-10cm long from the current season's growth.

1 *Trim with a sharp knife just below the leaf joint and remove the basal leaves.*

2 *Using a pencil or thin cane make a hole a few centimetres deep in a 7.5cm pot of moist cutting compost. Insert the cutting, firm the compost gently around the stem. Hormone rooting powder is not strictly necessary but the fungicide in this product will help to prevent rot. Do not cover the cutting as this encourages rotting. Place in a warm spot away from direct light and water sparingly to keep the compost moist. After two to three weeks when the roots have formed and the cuttings begin to grow, pot the cuttings on and move them into direct light.*

Cuttings also root in water; when roots are 5-7.5cm long, pot on carefully to avoid damaging young roots.

Pelargoniums need good light and grow happily on a bright sunny windowsill. In the growing season they enjoy moderate to hot conditions and are happy to spend summers outdoors once the danger of frost has passed. If temperatures and light levels allow, they will continue to grow throughout the winter, but where this is not the case, move them to a cool room for a winter rest and bring them out again in spring when growth recommences. One great bonus is that they thrive in dry air. Plants flower better when they are slightly potbound, but once roots begin to appear through the drainage holes, repot them in spring using John Innes No.2 compost with added horticultural grit to improve drainage.

Pinch out the growth tips of young plants to make them bushy and when plants have a winter rest, cut back the stems of mature plants by half in spring every year, just before they start into growth, otherwise they become spindly. Remove the flowering stems once the flowers have faded.

1

2

FEEDING AND WATERING

Overwatering is usually fatal, so water pelargoniums with care. Water moderately when plants are actively growing, allowing the compost surface to dry before rewatering. If plants are resting in winter, the compost should be very slightly moist; if conditions allow continuous growth, water as normal.

From spring, when they start to grow, until early autumn, when growth slows, feed pelargoniums every three weeks with a fertilizer for flowering houseplants.

PESTS AND PROBLEMS

Oedema: small wet corky patches appear on the leaves due to overwatering. Allow the compost to dry out and reduce watering.

'Blackleg' is a fungal growth that appears as a black patch at the base of the stem and is usually found on cuttings. Sterilize your knife in alcohol or methylated spirits before using it on other plants. Avoid cold or old compost and overwatering.

LONGEVITY

Pelargoniums can live for many years.

OTHER VARIETIES OF INTEREST
Zonal: The most commonly grown. Some are dwarf varieties, others are single, semi double or double-flowered, often with ornamental foliage.
Aromatic-foliaged geraniums: 'Prince of Orange' and 'Mabel Grey' have a strong lemon scent. 'Endsleigh' has a pepper scent and 'Little Gem' a spicy rose scent.

Above: Pelargonium graveolens *is grown for its delicately cut, citrus-scented foliage. The small flowers are white to pale pink.*

Below: *Pinch out the growing tips of young ivy-leaved, trailing stemmed varieties, such as this 'Mexicana', to encourage branching from the base.*

Left: *The large, soft pink-flowered regal pelargonium has the bonus of attractive foliage and is a taller, bushier plant than the small but floriferous 'mini-zonal'. Both are ideal plants for a windowsill or shelf.*

PEPEROMIA

These enchanting little plants exhibit an extraordinary variety of leaf colour and texture. Leaves may be puckered, smooth or hairy, with a wonderful selection of variegations. Many varieties produce unusual flower stems that project like wands above the foliage and are tipped with hundreds of tiny flowers. Their compact habit is perfect for positions where space is limited.

The native habitat of *Peperomia* is in the warmth and dappled light of the rainforest, so it is no surprise that when grown as a houseplant, it needs bright light with occasional sunshine, humidity and moderate to warm conditions in a draught-free position. Occasional misting with tepid water is sufficient, but increase the regularity if plants are growing in higher temperatures. Grouping plants together helps to maintain humidity. Varieties with fleshy leaves are more tolerant of dry air and will grow in centrally heated rooms, while those with smoother leaves need higher humidity. They will tolerate lower temperatures, but reduce watering and stop misting. Peperomias are shallow-rooted, so repotting is rarely necessary. Repot in spring only when the pot becomes packed with roots. Use a peat substitute-based mixture and water thoroughly.

Above: *Upright and trailing varieties, as well as variegated forms, are best propagated by tip cuttings. Detach a healthy shoot about 7.5cm long, trim below a leaf joint and remove the basal leaves. Dip the cutting in rooting powder and insert up to the leaf in compost.*

Above: *To make a leaf cutting, choose a healthy leaf and cut it off the plant leaving about 2.5cm of stalk. Insert it into cutting compost so that the stalk is almost completely in the compost, as shown below.*

Right: *This tray contains a selection of tip cuttings, leaf sections and whole leaf cuttings. Rooting should take about four to six weeks.*

PROPAGATION

All species can be propagated by tip cuttings taken between spring and early summer. Propagate variegated forms by shoot tip cuttings only; bushy varieties root from leaf cuttings.

Above: *Some peperomias, such as* P. argyreia, *grow from leaf sections, with the cut end inserted vertically in the cutting compost.*

FEEDING AND WATERING

Careful watering is the key to success. Use tepid water and allow the compost surface to dry slightly before rewatering. Beware of overwatering, which causes wilting and the collapse of plants. If this happens, do not water again until the surface has dried out. If the leaves suddenly fall, it is usually because of underwatering or low winter temperatures. Check the plant regularly and move it to a warmer room. Apply very little water in winter, just enough to keep the compost from shrinking. Feed with houseplant fertilizer every three weeks in summer and once or twice in winter.

PESTS AND PROBLEMS

Mealy bug can be an occasional problem.

Browning of the leaf tips and margins usually occurs if there has been a sudden drop in temperature. Move the plants away from draughts or the chill of a cold windowsill and remove damaged leaves.

LONGEVITY

Peperomias are not generally long-lived, but with care they can last for several years.

Right: *With its pale burgundy leaf undersides and dark surfaces marked with grey,* Peperomia obtusifolia *'Columbiana' creates an exotic air in a richly furnished room.*

Right: Peperomia obtusifolia *'USA' is a compact mass of cheerfully variegated leaves. Displayed singly or in groups on a bright windowsill, they are an uplifting sight.*

OTHER VARIETIES OF INTEREST

Peperomia argyreia, also seen as *Peperomia sandersii* (water melon peperomia): Marked with green and silver. Can be propagated from leaf cuttings.
Peperomia caperata: Dark green, heart-shaped leaves with wrinkled surface. Stems dark pink.
Peperomia clusiifolia: A tough little plant. Succulent leaves are green with a dark maroon margin.
Peperomia fraseri. May be labelled *P. resediflora:* White flowers on red stalks and patterned leaves.
Peperomia pereskifolia: Narrow succulent leaves around stiff stems.

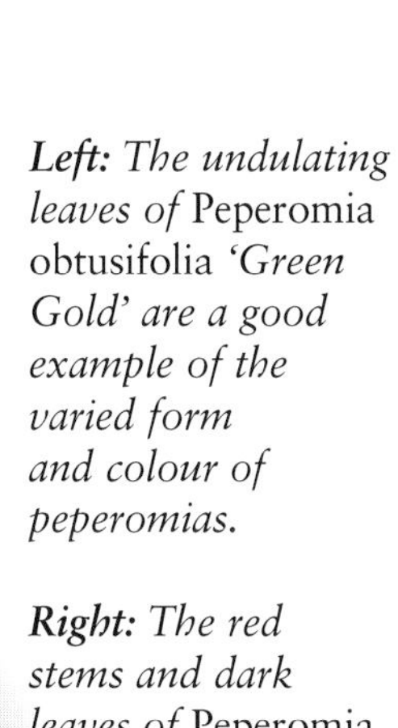

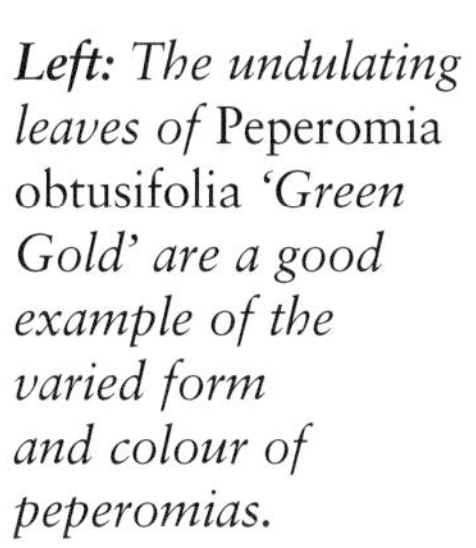

Left: *The undulating leaves of* Peperomia obtusifolia *'Green Gold' are a good example of the varied form and colour of peperomias.*

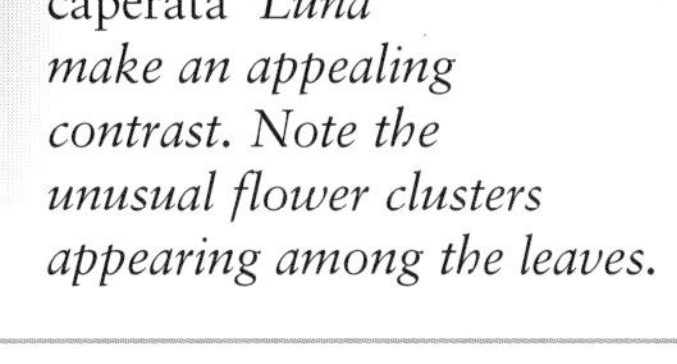

Right: *The red stems and dark leaves of* Peperomia caperata *'Luna' make an appealing contrast. Note the unusual flower clusters appearing among the leaves.*

PHILODENDRON

Philodendrons are grown for their eye-catching architectural foliage. The most common one is the sweetheart plant, so-called because of its heart-shaped bronze-tinted leaves, which become green as they mature. It is grown as a climber or with its stems draping from a hanging basket. Its large, spreading, non-climbing relatives with deeply lobed leaves need space to grow.

PROPAGATION

Propagate from 10-15cm-long tip cuttings in early summer, selecting a healthy shoot tip that includes a mature leaf from the current season's growth. Trim just below a leaf joint and remove the basal leaves.

1 *Make holes a few centimetres deep in a pot of moist cutting compost. If the leaves are large, cut them in half. Dip the base of the cutting in hormone rooting powder, gently tapping off the excess. Insert the cutting and firm the compost around the stem.*

2 *Place the pot in a loosely knotted plastic bag supported by canes and put it in a warm room away from direct light. Once the cuttings begin to grow, remove the bag, allow the cuttings to acclimatize for about a week and then pot them into separate containers.*

1

Although philodendrons need protection from direct summer sun, they are excellent for bright light or in partial shade. In winter, when light levels are low, move them as near to a window as possible. *Philodendron scandens* is the most shade-tolerant, surviving in poor light, while varieties with coloured leaves need brighter conditions. Temperatures should be constantly moderate. *P. scandens* is the most hardy, tolerating cool winter temperatures for short periods, particularly if the compost is almost dry.

The plants appreciate high humidity, particularly when they are actively growing or kept in heated rooms in winter. Mist large plants regularly with tepid water, particularly if they are growing up moss poles or supports. Mist smaller specimens or stand them on a tray of pebbles, filled almost to the base of the pot with water. Every two or three years in spring, repot plants into a container one size larger, using a peat-substitute mixture or John Innes No 2 compost. If plants are large and repotting is difficult, remove the top 5-7.5cm of compost each spring, replacing it with fresh material. Pinching out the growing tips of young plants encourages branching, but if they outgrow the available space, cut them back to encourage side growths. Bending the tip round and securing it at the base of the plant has the same effect. Aerial roots can be removed without harming the plant. Wipe the leaves regularly to keep them dust-free. To create a dense effect, it is a good idea to plant three plants in one pot.

2

It is worth noting that the sap contains a skin irritant and you should wear gloves when pruning or taking cuttings. However, do not let this discourage you from growing these magnificent plants.

FEEDING AND WATERING

Use tepid water and keep the plants moist but not waterlogged throughout the growing season. Allow the compost surface to dry out slightly between waterings. Keep the plants slightly moist in winter, but do not let them dry out completely. Feed fortnightly with a general houseplant fertilizer when the plant is actively growing and monthly during the winter.

PESTS AND PROBLEMS

Philodendrons are usually trouble-free, but may occasionally suffer from scale.

Erratic watering can cause yellowing of the leaves and browning of the tips. Check the compost by inserting your finger just below the surface. If it is dry, give the plant a thorough soaking, then water as normal. If it is too wet, allow the compost to dry out and begin watering again.

Direct sunlight can scorch the leaves, but if they look dull and lacklustre, give them more light.

LONGEVITY

Under ideal conditions, philodendrons can live for many years in the home.

OTHER VARIETIES OF INTEREST

Philodendron 'Emerald King': Mid-green leaves to 3cm long.
Philodendron 'Emerald Queen': Bright glossy green foliage.
Philodendron bipinnatifidum: (*P. selloum* is included in this species): Needs space; deeply cut, mature leaves up to 60cm long and 45cm across. Juvenile leaves are smaller and heart-shaped.
Philodendron erubescens 'Burgundy': A climber with arrow-shaped leaves, dark green above and red below.

Left: *P.* scandens *is happy to grow with its stems tumbling from a hanging basket. This allows you to appreciate the glossy heart-shaped leaves at their best.*

Right: *P. 'Medisa' has yellow-green mottled leaves and burgundy leaf stems and midribs. A well-grown specimen such as this looks stunning growing up a moss pole.*

Left: *P.* erubescens *'Imperial Red' has a regal appearance to match its name. The young, deep claret leaves mature to display a dark, deeply veined glossy surface.*

PILEA

Pilea cadierei is a colourful low-growing plant from the rainforests of Vietnam producing glossy green leaves marked with patches of metallic silver. It is one of a group of closely related houseplants renowned for their neatly patterned foliage. They vary in habit from bushy to trailing and make a fine mixed display in shallow pans or bowls. All of them are easy to grow.

Pileas are very tolerant and will survive in less than perfect conditions, but really appreciate bright light, moderate to warm conditions and constant humidity. Bright light or light shade, away from direct summer sunshine, ensures good leaf coloration. As light levels reduce, the strength of leaf colour decreases, so make sure that plants receive as much light as possible in winter. Pileas dislike draughts, but withstand periods at lower temperatures if watered sparingly. As with all houseplants, move them away from the windowsill on frosty nights, even if you have double glazing, as they are liable to be chilled. To maintain humidity, mist plants regularly with tepid water, group several plants together or stand them on a shallow tray of pebbles filled with water to just below the base of the pot.

As pileas have compact root systems, 7.5-10cm pots or shallow pans are ideal. Repot plants in spring, only if the compost is congested with roots, using a peat substitute-based compost and water them thoroughly. As they grow, pinch out the growing tips to keep plants bushy. Ageing plants naturally become straggly and lose their lower leaves, so repropagate them regularly.

1

2

3

PROPAGATION

Propagate pileas every two to three years. Cuttings can be taken at any time of year and root easily, but root most rapidly in late spring.

1 *Take 7.5-10cm-long shoot tip cuttings from healthy shoots of the current season's growth. Trim with a sharp knife just below the leaf joint and remove the basal leaves. Using a pencil or thin, cane make four holes a few centimetres deep in a 9cm pot of moist cutting compost.*
2 *Dip the base of the cuttings in hormone rooting powder if you have some, gently tap off the excess. Insert the cutting and firm the compost gently around the stem.*
3 *Place the pot in a loosely knotted plastic bag supported by four canes and put it in a warm spot away from direct light. Once roots are formed and the cuttings begin to grow, remove the bag, allow them to acclimatize for about a week and pot them into separate containers.*

Pileas also root easily in water. Simply suspend the cuttings in a jar of water. Pot up carefully to avoid damaging the roots

FEEDING AND WATERING

When plants are actively growing, water them with tepid water and keep the compost moist but never waterlogged. Allow the compost surface to dry out slightly between waterings. Feed every two weeks with a general houseplant fertilizer.

During the winter or when temperatures are low, water sparingly, but do not let the compost dry out. Feed monthly at this time.

PESTS AND PROBLEMS

Well cared for plants are generally trouble free but may suffer from aphids, or red spider mite in dry air. Check plants regularly, as small populations are easy to control. Isolate affected plants.

Leaf fall, particularly during winter, is usually as a result of overwatering, particularly in draughts or low temperatures. Bright sun and dry air can cause leaf curl; move the plant and increase humidity.

LONGEVITY

Plants are usually repropagated and replaced after two to three years.

OTHER VARIETIES OF INTEREST
Pilea cadierei 'Nana': A compact form of the aluminium plant.
Pilea involucrata 'Norfolk': Bronze leaves striped with silver.
Pilea microphylla: The artillery plant, so-called because of the explosive way in which mature flowers can expel a cloud of pollen over an area of 90cm or more. Succulent stems and tiny, bright, medium-green leaves arranged in flattened sprays, similar to the feathery fronds of ferns.
Pilea microphylla 'Variegata': small green leaves with pink and white markings.

Left: Pilea cadieri, *from the rainforests of Vietnam, has dark green leaves marked with silvery grey patches.*

Below: *The attractive and unusual bright green leaves of* Pilea *'Moon Valley' are textured and deeply veined.*

Below: Pilea involucrata *'Silver Tree' has an upright habit and very pleasing foliage. Pinch out the stems to encourage bushy growth.*

PLECTRANTHUS

This rapid grower makes an excellent specimen plant and is much admired for its masses of pretty leaves with their scalloped margins and irregular creamy white variegations. These are best appreciated when the trailing stems tumble over the sides of a hanging basket or a container on a pedestal. Thriving in bright light and warmth, they tolerate dry air and are easy to propagate.

A position in good bright light with some early morning or late afternoon sun throughout the year is ideal for 'Swedish ivy'. It tolerates a little shade, but needs as much light as possible in winter. If there is insufficient light, the leaf coloration weakens and fewer leaves are produced. Provide constantly warm conditions, except in winter, when a rest in moderate temperatures is beneficial. One great advantage of *Plectranthus* is that it tolerates a dry atmosphere and will grow in air-conditioned or centrally heated rooms. It is a fast-growing plant that is better repropagated annually or kept for a maximum of two to three years. Plants can be grown individually in 10-13cm pots or you can plant three or four in a hanging basket for a dense display of foliage. In either case, use John Innes No 2 compost. Pinch out the growth tips regularly from the main stems to encourage bushy growth. When older plants become straggly, cut them back to within a few centimetres of the base to generate new shoots.

1

2

PROPAGATION

Plectranthus will root easily whenever a leaf joint touches the compost. Layer in spring.

1 *Peg down some healthy shoots in a tray of moist compost and put the tray in a warm bright place.*
2 *Roots will grow from the leaf joints. Detach these rooted pieces from mid-spring to early summer, carefully easing them from the tray to avoid damaging the roots.*
3 *Pot the rooted pieces singly into 7.5cm pots of John Innes No 2 compost and pot them on as the compost becomes congested with roots.*

3

FEEDING AND WATERING

When the plants are actively growing, the compost should be constantly moist but never waterlogged. If the plant is overwintering in a cool room, reduce watering, keeping the compost slightly moist. From spring to autumn, feed every two weeks with a general liquid houseplant fertilizer. Reduce this to once every six to eight weeks in winter

PESTS AND PROBLEMS

Swedish ivy is usually problem-free, although fluctuating temperatures cause leaf drop.

LONGEVITY

Plants are better replaced every few years.

Left: Plectranthus australis *is plain green with beetroot-coloured stems and a similar coloration on some of the veins - an unusual combination.*

Below: Plectranthus coleoides *'Marginatus' grows into a bushy plant before its stems begin to trail over the side of the pot. This plant, like most of its relatives, dislikes any fluctuations in the temperature.*

Left: P. strigosus *is a stiff-stemmed plant with succulent, irregularly variegated leaves.*

AN ALTERNATIVE METHOD OF PROPAGATION

Plectranthus are easy to propagate from tip cuttings. Simply cut off a shoot about 7.5-10 cm long, trim below a leaf joint and remove the basal leaves. Dip the base of the cutting in hormone rooting powder and insert it in a pot of moist cutting compost.

RADERMACHERA

This is a relatively recent introduction that deserves wider recognition as a houseplant with style. Its deeply veined, glossy leaflets, with their finely tapering points, give the plant an air of refined elegance that is particularly evident in older specimens. Given good growing conditions, *Radermachera* develops rapidly. Its tolerance of dry air is an added advantage, making this a plant worthy of inclusion in any collection.

One factor that should establish the emerald tree's popularity is its tolerance of dry air and central heating, so that misting is not necessary. However, it dislikes fluctuating temperatures, draughts and overwatering, which will soon result in its demise. Give it good, bright light all year, away from scorching sunshine; plants suffer in low light levels. Conditions should be constantly cool to moderate throughout the year, and plants are happy to spend the summer outdoors in a bright sheltered position once there is no danger of frost. If the compost becomes congested with roots, repot the plant into a pot one size larger in spring, using a peat substitute-based compost or John Innes No 2 with added sharp sand or perlite to improve the drainage. If plants become spindly, prune them back in spring to within a few centimetres of the base and they will regrow.

PROPAGATION

Radermachera is easy to propagate from tip cuttings

1 *In spring, take a healthy 7.5-10cm-long shoot tip from the current season's growth. Trim with a sharp knife just below the leaf joint and remove the basal leaves.*

2 *Using a pencil or thin cane, make a hole a few centimetres deep in a 9cm pot of moist cutting compost. Dip the base of the cutting in hormone rooting powder, gently tapping off the excess. Insert the cutting and firm the compost around the stem.*

3 *Place the pot in a loosely knotted plastic bag supported by four canes and put it in a warm position away from direct light. Once roots are formed and the cutting begins to grow, remove the bag and allow the cutting to acclimatize for about a week before potting on as necessary.* Radermachera *can also be propagated by air layering.*

FEEDING AND WATERING

Use tepid water and keep the compost moist, allowing the surface to dry out between waterings. Do not overwater or allow the plant to stand in waterlogged compost. Feed actively growing plants every two weeks with a general liquid houseplant fertilizer. Do not feed if they are dormant in winter.

PESTS AND PROBLEMS

Mealy bug, whitefly and scale can affect *Radermachera*.

LONGEVITY

With correct care and careful watering, *Radermachera* plants can last for many years in the home.

OTHER VARIETIES OF INTEREST
Radermachera sinica 'Kaprima': A variegated form with pale greenish yellow margins.

Left: Radermachera sinica. *The glossy dark green leaflets of this well-kept specimen certainly help the plant to live up to its common name, the emerald tree.*

Below: *A close look at the rich green leaflets reveals their delicate nature, and sunlight streaming through the plant often highlights the fine tracery of their veins. This is certainly a magnificent plant.*

RHODODENDRON

The azalea is one of the most spectacular flowering houseplants, renowned for the sheer number of blooms that clothe the bush for several weeks in winter, at a time when few plants are in flower. To prolong the flowering season, buy this dense, compact plant with small leathery leaves when it is massed with buds and has a few open flowers. With care, it can be retained to flower in successive years.

PROPAGATION

Cuttings take root easily; use them to replace older plants.

1 *In spring, take healthy 7.5-10cm-long shoot tips from the new growth. Trim them with a sharp knife just below a leaf joint and remove the basal leaves.*

2 *Using a pencil or thin cane, make four holes a few centimetres deep in a 9cm pot of moist cutting compost. Dip the base of each cutting in hormone rooting powder, gently tapping off the excess. Insert the cuttings and firm the compost around the stem.*

3 *Place the pot in a loosely knotted plastic bag supported by canes, and put it in a warm, bright position. Once roots are formed and the cuttings begin to grow, remove the bag, allow them to acclimatize for a week and pot into separate containers.*

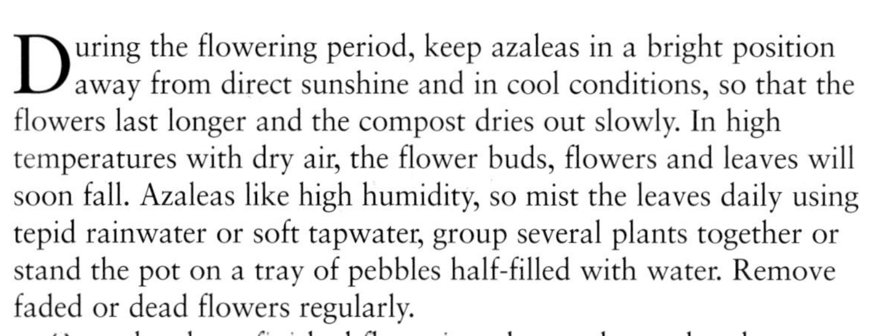

During the flowering period, keep azaleas in a bright position away from direct sunshine and in cool conditions, so that the flowers last longer and the compost dries out slowly. In high temperatures with dry air, the flower buds, flowers and leaves will soon fall. Azaleas like high humidity, so mist the leaves daily using tepid rainwater or soft tapwater, group several plants together or stand the pot on a tray of pebbles half-filled with water. Remove faded or dead flowers regularly.

Once they have finished flowering, do not throw the plants away, but keep them to flower the following year. Most plants are potbound, so repot them into a container one size larger, using compost for acid-loving plants. Water the plant thoroughly and place it in a bright position in a cool, frost-free room. Continue feeding and watering, allowing the compost surface to become just dry before rewatering. Once the danger of frost is past, azaleas can spend the summer outside in a cool, partially shaded position under the dappled light of a large shrub or at the base of a shady wall. If the soil in your garden is acidic, bury the pot to the level of the compost surface. Water, feed and mist the plant throughout the summer, and in early autumn, before the first frosts, bring it indoors into a cool room or glasshouse. Keep the plant cool while it is in bud and once the first flowers open, move it to its display position. Repeat the same process annually, repotting into a container one size larger every two to three years.

FEEDING AND WATERING

Keep the compost thoroughly moist at all times using soft water or tepid rainwater. If this is impossible and your tapwater is hard, add half-strength liquid feed for acid-loving plants or sequestrine each time you water. To water, plunge the pot into a container of water and allow the excess to drain away. Feed once every two weeks from spring to early autumn with a liquid fertilizer formulated for acid-loving plants.

PESTS AND PROBLEMS

Red spider mite and mealy bug can affect azaleas.

Brown leaf tips and margins followed by shrivelling are caused by underwatering, dry air, excessive heat, or too much sunshine.

Yellowing leaves are caused by lime in the compost, water or fertilizer; use soft water, rainwater or add a half-strength ericaceous fertilizer at each watering.

LONGEVITY

With correct care, adequate watering and regular feeding, your azalea plant will flower for many seasons.

Above: *The pink-and-white flowers of* Rhododendron *'Inga' look as if they were made from tissue paper.*

Above: *This is a novel idea, a 'standard' rhododendron that can be used as a specimen plant or to add height to a group display.*

Left: Rhododendron *'Rosali', a shell-pink flowered beauty, is ideal as a specimen plant, particularly when set against a dark background that emphasizes the flower colours.*

SAINTPAULIA

With their vibrant flower colours and neat, compact habit, it is little wonder that these plants, whose origins are in the Tanzanian rainforest, have charmed their way into so many homes. Ideal where space is limited, they are equally effective whether displayed alone, in groups or alongside other houseplants. Given adequate light, humidity and moist compost, they will flower all year.

African violets prefer moderate to warm conditions; if you do not feel chilly, neither will they. As with many houseplants, move them from the windowsill on cold winter nights. Unless the air is extremely dry, African violets will survive and flower moderately without increased humidity, but for them to flourish and flower profusely, additional humidity helps. Either display them in groups so that moist air is trapped between the leaves or stand them on pebbles in a tray of water. Top up the water constantly to achieve the best results. If you prefer to mist plants, ensure that the spray is as fine as possible. Too little light is the main reason for lack of flowers. If this is the case, move the plants to a brighter position, but not into direct sunshine, which is too strong and damaging. If winter light levels are low, you can encourage flowering by suspending a twin-tube fluorescent light fitting with, one 'cool white' and one 'warm white' tube 30cm above the plants for 12-16 hours each day. Depending on the speed of growth, the plants will need repotting every two years using a peat substitute-based compost. Do not use too large a pot.

1

3

2

PROPAGATION

African violets are among the easiest plants to propagate from leaf cuttings.

1 *Choose a healthy leaf and remove it with a sharp knife or break it off cleanly. Trim the stalk to 2.5cm, making a diagonal cut to increase the area where the new roots will be produced.*
2 *Using a dibber, make holes in moist peat-substitute cutting mixture and insert the leaf cuttings until they are level with the surface; firm gently.*
3 *Insert the pot into a loosely knotted plastic bag supported with four canes.*
4 *Plantlets appear at the base of the leaves in 12-16 weeks, so be patient. Pot on into 9cm pots; do not compact the compost. Water well.*

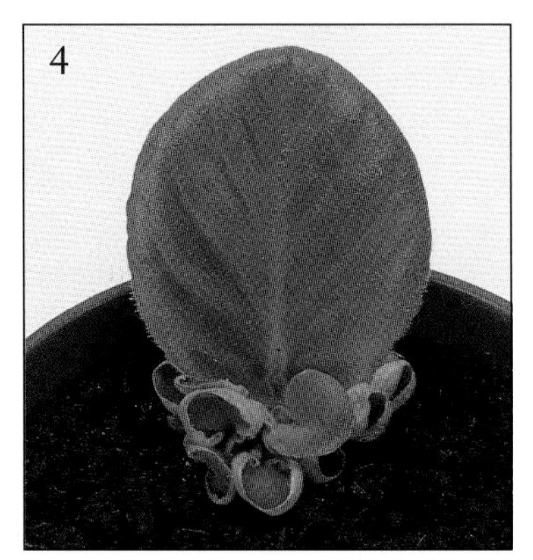
4

FEEDING AND WATERING

Use tepid water and do not splash water on the leaves, as this may cause scorching or the appearance of grey mould. If water should splash, soak it off the leaf with absorbent paper. Use a watering can with a narrow nozzle and push it through the leaves to the compost or stand the pot in 5cm of water for 30 minutes before draining it. Overwatering is a common cause of failure. Water when the compost surface has dried out or the leaves start to wilt a little. Feed monthly in summer with a high-potash fertilizer.

PESTS AND PROBLEMS

Spray whitefly, usually found on the undersides of leaves, with permethrin. Dab mealy bugs - white, waxy creatures - with a paintbrush dipped in methylated or surgical spirits and wipe them off carefully.

LONGEVITY

African violets can survive as houseplants for ten years and, in exceptional cases, for 20 or even 30 years.

Above: *Mini African violets are much smaller than their cousins, so you are bound to find space for one or two in your collection.*

Right: *You can make a richly coloured display by grouping several plants together and creating a mass of velvety flowers and leaves.*

Below: *'Tineke' is one of a stunning new group of candy-striped African violets known as 'chimeras' that plant breeders are currently developing.*

Left: *The rich cerise pink of S. 'Ramona' is a long way removed from the pale blue flowers of the wild species. Note the superbly healthy, dark green leaves.*

SANSEVIERIA

This is a slow-growing, statuesque plant with many virtues, forgiving in the extreme and with a robust nature that survives the worst excesses of a busy gardener. Resolute in the face of neglect, erratic watering, dry air, sunshine, shade or draughts, it is easy to grow, but happier given care and attention. Plants rarely need repotting and overwatering is the most common cause of death.

Sansevierias are happiest in bright light with some sunshine. Although they tolerate lower light levels, their growth slows, and in very deep shade, it almost stops. Never transfer your plant suddenly from shade to sunshine, but allow it time to acclimatize to the new conditions for a few hours over several days before the final move. Moderate to warm room conditions are ideal, but with careful watering, the plants tolerate temperatures to just above freezing and grow happily outdoors in summer. Dry air is not a problem, but plants appreciate occasional misting with tepid water.

There is no need to repot mother-in-law's tongue until it is really potbound. You can even wait until the container cracks; it certainly makes extracting the plants easier! Use clay pots, if possible, for greater stability and repot in late spring into a pot one size larger. Put a good layer of pot fragments, grit or polystyrene granules in the bottom to help drainage. Use John Innes No 2 compost and mix in a little sharp sand and peat substitute. In the years when plants are not repotted, topdress them by carefully removing and replacing the top 5-7.5cm of compost. Keep the leaves clean by wiping them gently with a damp cloth.

1

2

3

PROPAGATION BY DIVISION

You can divide plants in spring when you repot them.

1. *Remove the plant from the pot and separate the rooting offsets by easing the sections apart or cutting them off at the base with a sharp knife or even an old hacksaw - they can be very tough.*
2. *Make sure that each offset has well-developed roots .*
3. *Repot them in the same compost mixture used for adult plants. Stand the pots in a bright position and water sparingly until established.*

FEEDING AND WATERING

Water regularly from spring to autumn, allowing the compost surface to dry out between watering. Avoid waterlogging, which is particularly easy with plants growing in the shade or at low winter temperatures, when the compost should be almost dry. However, plants also suffer if underwatered. Feed every three weeks during the growing season with a general houseplant fertilizer.

PESTS AND PROBLEMS

Leaves yellowing, becoming soft and dying back are signs of basal rot, usually due to overwatering. If only part of the plant is affected, divide it, throw away the affected parts and keep the healthy section. Dust cuts with fungicide and repot. Keep the plant dry in a warm position.

Sunken red-brown spots with yellow margins are evidence of fungal infection. Avoid wetting the foliage and remove badly affected leaves.

LONGEVITY

With their slow growth and resilience, sansevierias can last for many years, even in difficult conditions.

MOTHER-IN-LAW'S TONGUE

Below: Sansevieria trifasciata *'Laurentii' has long leaves and narrow yellow margins. 'Golden Futura' is similar, but broader-leaved, while 'Golden Hahnii', sometimes called the golden bird's nest, produces low-growing rosettes with broad margins.*

OTHER VARIETIES OF INTEREST

S. trifasciata 'Compacta': Similar characteristics to 'Laurentii', but a smaller plant.
S. t. 'Craigii': Similar to 'Laurentii' but with paler bands and several vertical streaks.
S. t. 'Moonshine': An attractive variety with silvery green foliage.
S. t. 'Silver Hahnii': Grey-green leaves with dark stripes.

PROPAGATION BY LEAF CUTTINGS

You can propagate the ordinary form of *Sansevieria trifasciata* by leaf cuttings, but be sure to propagate the yellow-variegated 'Laurentii' by division (shown on page 118) to retain the attractive edges to its leaves.

1 *Choose a healthy leaf and cut it off at the base.*
2 *Using a sharp knife, cut the leaf cleanly into sections about 5cm long.*
3 *Fill a pot with equal parts of moist peat substitute-based compost and sharp sand. Push each section into the mixture and firm gently.*
4 *Water the cuttings with tepid water and allow to drain. Each cutting will sprout roots and bear fresh new leaves.*

1

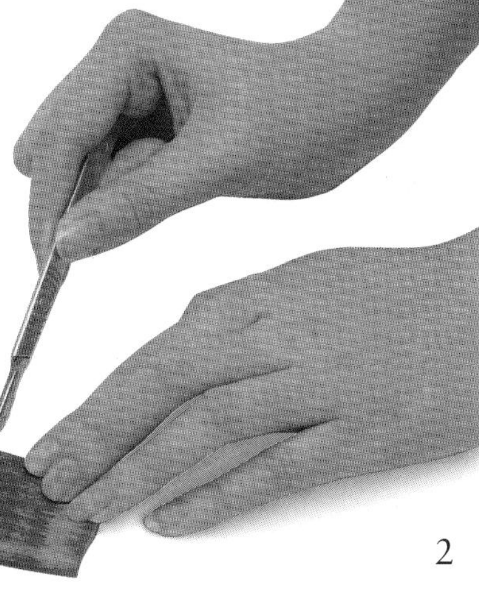

2

3

4

MOTHER OF THOUSANDS

SAXIFRAGA

This saxifrage has long been popular for its delicate charm and tolerance of cool conditions. The loose rosettes of hairy, mid-green leaves with silvery veins are complemented by masses of slender red stems bearing baby plantlets that drape from the pot like an elegant curtain. Grow them in a hanging basket or a pot on a pedestal, where their graceful beauty can be fully appreciated.

Saxifrages thrive in bright light and need some direct sunlight to keep the leaf coloration strong; if they are grown in poor light, the colour soon fades. They are a great asset to houseplant collectors for their tolerance of cool to moderate conditions but be sure to protect them from frost during the winter and keep them well ventilated at higher summer temperatures. Mist the leaves occasionally with a light spray of tepid water, particularly if they are growing in a hanging basket, or stand the pot on a tray of pebbles filled with water to just below the base of the pot. Misting is particularly important at higher temperatures.

Repot plants in spring, every one or two years when the compost becomes congested with roots. Use a pot one size larger and John Innes No 2, with a layer of broken clay pot fragments or polystyrene chippings in the bottom of the pot to improve drainage. Water thoroughly after repotting.

PROPAGATION

In spring or early summer, detach several good sized plantlets and peg them into a pot of John Innes No 2 compost, put them in a bright or lightly shaded warm position and water the compost sufficiently to keep it slightly moist. The plantlets should root in a few weeks and can be potted on and treated as adult plants. Alternatively, peg the plantlets into the compost while they are still attached to the parent plant, keep the compost slightly moist and detach them from the parent plant once they have rooted. Large plants can be divided at repotting time.

FEEDING AND WATERING

Keep the compost moist during the growing season, allowing the surface to dry out between each watering. The plants are particularly vulnerable to waterlogging, so water with care, especially in winter, when the compost should be kept only slightly moist.

Feed with a general liquid houseplant fertilizer every two weeks during the growing season and once or twice during the winter.

PESTS AND PROBLEMS

In poor light the stems become spindly; move the plant into a brighter position. Low temperatures or dry air also cause poor growth.

Aphids may occasionally be a problem.

LONGEVITY

After a few years, older plants become straggly and should be repropagated. Younger plants are more vigorous and produce more plantlets.

***Left:** The simplest propagation method is to peg out the plantlets (detail photograph) while attached to the parent.*

***Left:** The dark green hairy leaves of* Saxifraga stolonifera *bear a radiating pattern of delicate pale veins. Their subdued appearance provides a distinct contrast to those of the variegated variety.*

***Below:** The leaves of* S. stolonifera *'Tricolor' have green and cream variegations that are accompanied, and sometimes overtaken, by a beautiful rose-coloured flush. It is slow-growing and needs warmer winter temperatures.*

Right: Saxifraga stolonifera *has pretty leaves with attractive markings and raspberry-coloured undersides that are covered with pink hairs when young.*

SCHEFFLERA

These magnificent upright foliage plants are prized for their decorative leathery leaves, which radiate from stiff leaf stalks like the multiple spokes of a glossy umbrella. Several specimens planted in a large container and trained up bamboo canes or a moss pole create a stunning architectural display. They richly earn their place in any houseplant collection.

Umbrella plants need a brightly lit or lightly shaded position throughout the year. Turn them regularly to ensure that all sides of the plant receive adequate light. As they dislike draughts or fluctuations in temperature, keep them in moderate to warm conditions at all times. If watered sparingly, they will tolerate slightly lower temperatures in winter. They also prefer constant humidity, so group smaller plants together with other houseplants, mist them regularly with tepid water or stand them on a tray of pebbles filled with water almost to the base of the container. Misting is the only practical option for larger specimens.

Repot scheffleras annually in spring, using a peat substitute-based mixture or John Innes No 2 compost. (Being loam-based, John Innes composts are heavier and give taller plants greater stability.) Gently tease away the old compost from among the roots. Water thoroughly after repotting, but take care not to overwater, as repotted plants are particularly sensitive to this. Once they reach their maximum pot size, top- dress the plants every year by removing and replacing the top 5-7.5cm of compost and ensure that they are well fed and watered. Three or four plants in a pot create a denser effect than single specimens. Tie tall plants to bamboo canes or moss poles to keep the main stem straight and well supported. If they outgrow their position or become straggly, prune near to the base in spring and use the tips as cuttings. Removing the growing tips from smaller plants encourages bushiness and makes for a well-shaped plant.

Sponge the leaves every few weeks with tepid water to remove dust. If you can provide a position sheltered from scorching sunshine and wind, the plants will enjoy a late spring and summer holiday outdoors, but remember to bring them indoors before the first frosts. Since their sap can cause dermatitis, avoid touching the cut ends when taking cuttings or pruning.

1

PROPAGATION

Take tip cuttings in spring.

1 *Select a healthy 7.5-10cm-long shoot tip from the current season's growth and trim it just below the leaf joint. Remove the basal leaves; if the remaining leaves are large, cut them in half.*

2 *Make a shallow hole in a 9cm pot of moist cutting compost. Dip the base of the cutting in hormone rooting powder, tap off the excess, insert the cutting and firm it in gently. Place the pot in a loosely knotted plastic bag supported by four canes and put it in a warm corner away from direct light. Once the cutting begins to grow, remove the bag, allow it to acclimatize for about a week and then pot it on.*

2

FEEDING AND WATERING

Water thoroughly from spring to autumn, allowing the compost surface to dry out between waterings. When the plants are growing actively in summer, feed fortnightly with a general houseplant fertilizer. Water sparingly in winter and feed monthly. Waterlogging is a common cause of death.

PESTS AND PROBLEMS

Scheffleras are generally trouble-free, but may suffer from red spider mite if conditions are too warm and dry. Check plants regularly for aphids and scale insect.

Scorched or bleached leaves are caused by excess light. Brown patches on the leaves and leaf margins that turn brown are caused by dry air; increase humidity.

Leaf fall is caused by low temperatures and waterlogging. Move plants to a warmer room and cease watering. If the leaves become lacklustre and lose colour, it is a sign that they need more light or food.

LONGEVITY

If well cared for, plants can last for many years. Some reach a considerable height.

UMBRELLA TREE

***Below:** As its name indicates,* S. arboricola *'Compacta' has a dense growth habit. Here, several plants are growing up a moss pole for greater impact.*

Right: S. arboricola *'Trinette' is a delightful form with dark green foliage and bright yellow markings on many of the leaflets.*

***Right:** The broad glossy leaflets of* Schefflera *'Amate' do not need colourful variegation to attract the eye. Their size and bold architectural appearance makes them ideal specimen plants.*

OTHER VARIETIES OF INTEREST

S. actinophylla (formerly *Brassaia actinophylla*) octopus tree: Leathery, glossy leaves that look lacquered when young. Grows to 1.8-2.5m tall.

S. arboricola (also labelled *Heptapleurum arboricola*): Dainty, compact habit and narrow leaves.

S. a. 'Gold Capella': Deep green leaflets with golden splashes.

S. a. 'Janine': Yellow variegation and undulating leaflets with scalloped margins.

S. a. 'Nora': Bushy in growth with glossy green leaflets.

S. a. 'Renata': Dark green leaves with undulating scalloped margins.

S. a. 'Sofia': Mid-green foliage with irregular yellow margins.

S. digitata: A smaller variety than *S. actinophylla.*

S. heptaphylla (also labelled *Schefflera octophylla*): Distinct veining on the leaflets.

SINNINGIA

It is hard to resist the temptation to touch the beautiful, velvety textured flowers of sinningias, projecting like clusters of bells from the centre of the plant. As single specimens, the plants are spectacular, but group several together and their presence is regal. The large, paddle-shaped leaves have deep, prominent veins; choose a plant with healthy leaves and plenty of flower buds.

1

2

3

Southern Brazil, with its wet and dry seasons, is the home of sinningia's ancestors and provides a clue to the conditions the plants require, namely bright, filtered light, a warm, draught-free position, high humidity and moist compost. To keep the atmosphere humid, stand the plant on some pebbles in a tray of water, making sure the water does not touch the bottom of the pot. Alternatively, mist the air around the plant with a fine spray, but take care, as water marks the leaves and flowers.

Do not throw away sinningias when flowering is over - it's such a waste! Imagine that it is their 'dry season'; as the leaves begin to yellow, gradually reduce watering, stop feeding, allow the compost to dry out and then store the pot in a cool place. In spring, repot the tuber, hollow side up, level with the surface of a peat substitute-based compost. Begin watering, sparingly at first, increasing the amount as the leaves grow; once they are about 7.5cm long, you can begin to feed the plant every two weeks until the end of the flowering season and move it back on display.

PROPAGATION

If you like a challenge, you can try growing sinningias from seed, but the seedlings are tiny and prone to fungal diseases. Sow the seed in spring onto the surface of a finely sieved seed compost and put the tray in a warm propagator, keeping the humidity high. Once the seeds germinate, pot them into seed trays or pots and maintain the warm conditions; it takes six months from seed to flowering.

Another method is to divide large tubers, each with a single bud, as they are coming into growth. Dust the cuts with fungicide and replant into peat-substitute based compost.

The simplest and most successful method of propagating sinningias is by leaf cuttings.

1 *Select a healthy leaf from a vigorous plant and cut it into sections 5cm wide.*
2 *Fill a pot or seed tray with equal parts of moist peat-based compost and sharp sand or vermiculite. Make a slit 7.5-10cm deep, insert the base of the cutting and firm the compost.*
3 *Cover the tray with a plastic cover or plastic bag, place it in a warm spot and ventilate it occasionally. Pot on plantlets as necessary.*

FEEDING AND WATERING

Sinningias are fussy about water; it should be soft and at room temperature. Never allow the compost to become waterlogged; water carefully until you have gauged just how much the plant needs.

Feed fortnightly until the end of the flowering season with a fertilizer for flowering houseplants.

PESTS AND PROBLEMS

Aphids and red spider mite may affect the plants.

Yellow leaves indicate lack of food, draughts or chilling.

LONGEVITY

Sinningias can live for several years, but require care and attention to flourish.

Other varieties of interest

Sinningias are divided into two main groups. The Fyfiana group have large, bell-shaped flowers and spotted or blotched throats, such as 'Mont Blanc' with white flowers and 'Violacea' with deep purple-blue flowers. The Maxima group have nodding flowers; try 'Pink Slipper' with its pink flowers and spotted throat.

Above: *The double crimson flowers and white margins of 'Gregor Mendel' are particularly eye-catching.*

Below: *Some sinningias have beautifully speckled flowers, so there will certainly be one variety to suit your taste.*

Left: *The flowers of this* Sinningia *cultivar have a spectacularly rich colour scheme: pale raspberry with a deep crimson throat.*

SOLANUM

These compact little plants are grown for their cheerful winter fruits. Tiny white flowers appear in summer and are followed by long-lasting berries that ripen in autumn, gradually colouring through green to yellow before turning to bright orange-red like tiny tomatoes. Jerusalem and winter cherries are usually disposed of once the berries deteriorate, but they can be kept for several seasons.

Jerusalem and winter cherries need bright light and some sunshine, particularly through autumn and winter when they are fruiting, but take care not to expose plants to scorching summer sunshine. A cool to moderately warm room is preferable, as the combination of dry air and high temperatures found in centrally heated rooms considerably reduces the life of the berries. Mist plants daily with tepid water - more often in a warm room - or stand pots on a tray or saucer of pebbles filled with water almost to the base of the pot.

If you are keeping plants for another year, give them a rest in a cool room from late winter until early spring, watering sparingly, and then repot the plant into a pot one size larger, using John Innes No 2 compost. When there is no danger of frost, prune back the main stems to half or two-thirds their length, just above a leaf and put the pot in a bright sheltered spot outdoors, where the small white summer flowers can be pollinated by insects. Tapping the stems to shake out the pollen and misting the flowers also helps pollination. As the stems develop, pinch out the tips just above a leaf to encourage bushy growth. Mist, feed and water the plants throughout the summer, then bring them indoors into a cool to moderately warm room before the first frosts, for the fruits to ripen. It is worth noting that all parts of the plant are poisonous.

***Right:** You can collect your own seed simply by splitting the ripe berries open and teasing out the seeds. Let them dry and sow them in early spring to produce plants and a new crop of berries in the same growing season.*

They resemble tomato seeds

PROPAGATION

In spring, sow seeds 1.25cm apart and just below the surface of moist John Innes seed compost. Place the tray in a plastic bag or propagator and stand it in bright, indirect light until the seeds germinate two to three weeks later. Once they have germinated, remove the cover, keep them warm and when they are large enough to handle, pot them on into 7.5cm pots. Repot the plants as the compost becomes congested with roots and pinch out the tips to encourage bushy growth.

Seed sown in early spring produces flowers and fruit the same year.

FEEDING AND WATERING

Keep the compost moist but not waterlogged. Use tepid water and allow the surface of the compost to dry out between waterings. When the plant is actively growing, feed every two weeks with a general houseplant fertilizer, but only once a month in low temperatures. Use a flowering houseplant fertilizer for those plants that you wish to keep for future years.

PESTS AND PROBLEMS

Check plants regularly, as small populations of pests are easy to control, and isolate affected plants. Aphids can spread rapidly and whitefly can be a problem. Red spider mite are often associated with dry air.

Leaf fall in late winter is quite natural, but at any other time it usually indicates overwatering. Dropping berries are generally a sign of too little light, high temperatures or hot dry air. Move the plants to a cooler, brighter position.

LONGEVITY

Jerusalem and winter cherries will last several years before they need repropagating.

Left: Capsicum annuum *is a relative of winter cherries. Many varieties are grown for their coloured fruits, here a subtle cream, which last for several weeks in bright, cool to moderate surroundings.*

Right: An orange capsicum. These plants are commonly known as sweet peppers. Check regularly for pests.

Left: The Jerusalem cherry, Solanum pseudocapsicum, *is almost identical to the winter, or Christmas, cherry. Its white flowers are followed by berries that are attractive at all the stages of ripening, finally turning bright orange.*

Right: This capsicum has unusual dark purple fruits. Pinch out the tips to encourage bushy growth and mist plants regularly to keep them healthy.

SOLEIROLIA

Valued by some people and regarded as a garden weed by others, baby's tears, or mind-your-own-business, is an extremely vigorous creeping plant, with a spread as relentless as the incoming tide. Creating a dense mass of minute fresh green foliage, it foams over a pot or shallow tray and also makes an attractive covering around the base of tall plants. It is easy to care for and propagate.

A bright, cool position with constant humidity is perfect for this plant, although it is tolerant of less than perfect conditions. It will survive in most light levels, providing it is shaded from scorching sun. Although it tolerates a wide range of temperatures, almost down to freezing, ideally they should be moderate to low and never too high, particularly if the atmosphere is dry. High humidity keeps growth fresh and vigorous, so mist plants regularly with tepid water or stand them on a shallow tray of pebbles half filled with water.

Repot *Soleirolia* as necessary in spring into 10-15cm pots or shallow trays. Use John Innes No.1 compost and water thoroughly. As propagation is so simple, it is better to repropagate regularly and replace existing plants once they have outgrown their container.

PROPAGATION

Soleirolia is a very easy plant to propagate by simple division.

1 Carefully remove small clumps, 5-8cm square, complete with roots, from an established plant.

2 Put them into fresh compost and water them thoroughly.

3 Maintain high humidity and keep them in light partial shade until they are established. Once new growth appears, move the cuttings to a permanent position. As they are so easy to propagate, why not let your children have a go at raising their first 'new' plant.

1

2

3

FEEDING AND WATERING

Keep the compost moist but not waterlogged. Use tepid water. As watering from above can cause rotting, it is better to water from the base, pouring away the excess after about an hour. Do not leave the pot standing in water. Feed with a general liquid houseplant fertilizer every three to four weeks when they are actively growing and once or twice during winter.

PESTS AND PROBLEMS

Soleirolias are generally trouble-free. Dry compost or air causes withering and irregular watering causes loss of leaves or leaf spotting.

LONGEVITY

The plants live for many years but are usually repropagated because they outgrow their container.

BABY'S TEARS

Left: *You can buy plants trained through a tube to give a treelike effect. It is a novel way of growing them and is certain to puzzle and fascinate your friends.*

Below: *Grouping several varieties together has a greater impact than displaying one plant on its own.*

Soleirolia soleirolii *'Aurea'. The golden yellow leaf coloration is stronger in bright light. (Also sold as 'Golden Queen')*

Soleirolia soleirolii. *Masses of tiny, round, mid-green leaves and insignificant white flowers. (Formerly known as* Helxine soleirolii)

Soleirolia soleirolii *'Variegata' with silvery-white leaf margins. (Also sold as 'Argentea' or 'Silver Queen')*

SOLENOSTEMON

These highly decorative plants, formerly known as *Coleus blumei,* are easy to propagate and care for. Grown for their ornamental foliage, flame nettles are available in a wide range of tints, shades and often dazzling patterns. Adding to the overall effect, the leaf margins may be scalloped, serrated or fringed. These plants develop quickly and are fascinating for children to grow.

The strength of leaf coloration in the flame nettles depends on light levels; in good light it is strong, but where light levels are low or during the winter, the colour fades and then returns as the daylength and light quality increases. Flame nettles need as much bright light as possible and enjoy some direct sunshine, although light shading in summer is essential. Conditions should remain constantly warm to moderate and draught-free throughout the year, and as the plants dislike dry air, they need regular misting with tepid water. Alternatively, stand the plants on a shallow tray of pebbles filled with water to just below the base of the pot.

Repot young plants regularly as they develop and once they are established, repot them annually in spring using a peat substitute-compost or John Innes No 2. As the plants grow, pinch out the growing tips every two or three weeks to encourage branching and to stop the flowers forming. This also prevents plants from becoming leggy and defoliated. If they become spindly with age, prune them back in spring, cutting back the older stems to promote new growth.

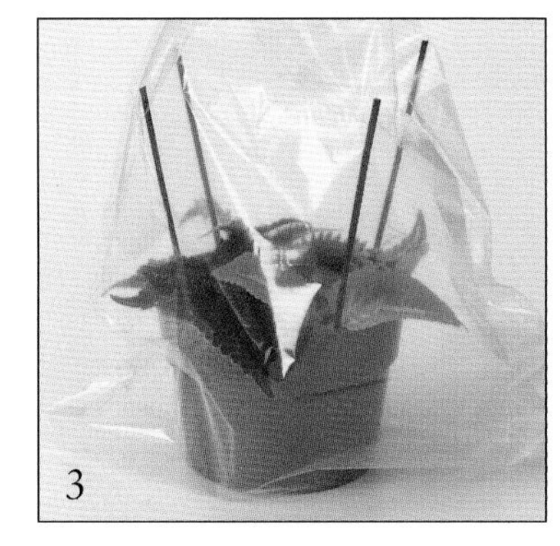

3

1

2

PROPAGATION

Take 7.5-10cm-long shoot tip cuttings from non-flowering shoots in spring or summer.

1 *Trim with a sharp knife just below the leaf joint and remove the basal leaves.*

2 *Make four holes a few centimetres deep in a 9cm pot of moist cutting compost. If the leaves are large, cut them in half. Dip the base of the cuttings in hormone rooting powder, gently tap off the excess and insert the cuttings. Firm the compost gently around the stem.*

3 *Place the pot in a loosely knotted plastic bag, supported by four canes and put it in a warm corner away from direct light. Cuttings root in two to three weeks. Once the cuttings begin to grow, remove the bag, allow them to acclimatize for a week and pot them into separate containers. Water them just enough to moisten the potting mixture, allowing the top 1.25cm to dry out between waterings until the plants are established.*

Cuttings root easily in water. Plants can also be grown from seeds sown in spring.

FEEDING AND WATERING

Using tepid water, keep the compost constantly moist when plants are actively growing, but beware of waterlogging, particularly at lower temperatures. Reduce watering in winter but do not let the compost become too dry, as the sappy leaves and stems soon collapse. Feed every two weeks in summer with a general liquid houseplant fertilizer, but only once or twice during winter.

PESTS AND PROBLEMS

Aphids may be a problem.

Wilting and falling leaves can be caused by low temperatures, lack of water or low humidity. Some leaves are naturally shed as winter approaches.

LONGEVITY

Flame nettles are usually grown as annuals but can be kept for several years.

Below: *A group of flame nettles makes an impressive display. There are many superb colour varieties to choose. Most of the plants sold in garden centres are seed raised; named varieties are available from specialist nurseries.*

VARIETIES OF INTEREST

'Brilliant': Crimson red leaves with golden yellow edges.
'Candidus': Central white patch in pale green leaves.
'Golden Bedder': Lemon yellow, deepening to gold.
'Sabre': Dwarf with long sword-shaped, muticoloured leaves.
Fancy leaf margins, such as ruffled: 'The Chief'; frilly: 'Firebird'; wavy: 'Butterfly'.
Single-coloured: 'Volcano', deep red.
Multicoloured: 'Scarlet Poncho', 'Milky Way'.
Trailing: *S. pumilus, S. rehneltianus.*

SPATHIPHYLLUM

The glossy green, lance-shaped leaves of *Spathiphyllum* display their stately elegance throughout the year, a perfect complement to the long-lasting waxen flower heads that gradually unfurl like billowing white sails, becoming delicately flushed with pale green as they age. They flourish in warm conditions; in a less favourable position they produce fewer flowers.

To achieve the best results, spathiphyllums need bright light, constant warmth and humidity. However, in common with many houseplants, they are very tolerant and will survive in partial shade and moderate temperatures, although growth is slower and there will be fewer flowers. Keep spathiphyllums away from scorching sun in summer but near a window in winter, when light levels and day length are reduced. Spathiphyllums prefer a constantly warm, draught-free position and although they tolerate temperature variations, at constant low temperatures growth is sparse and slow. Provide high humidity in spring and summer, but reduce it in winter unless the plant is in a heated room. In this case, mist it regularly or stand the pot on a tray of pebbles half filled with water. In lower light and temperatures, reduce humidity. Depending on the growing conditions, the flowers, which last more than six weeks, may appear at any time, although they are more common from spring to autumn. Remove them when they deteriorate. Repot plants each spring using a peat substitute-based mixture and water thoroughly. Once they are in a 15-18cm pot, lift and prune the roots back by one third before repotting the plant back into the same container but with new potting mixture.

1

2

3

PROPAGATION

Peace lilies can be divided in spring when you are repotting the parent plant.

1 *Divide plants by gently pulling apart the rhizomes. Each piece should have two to three leaves and a good root system.*
2 *Plant each piece in a peat substitute-based mixture at the same depth as the parent plant. Water thoroughly.*
3 *Move the plantlets into the shade until they are established and do not feed them for three months. Establishment can be slow if temperatures are low. Avoid overwatering the new plants.*

FEEDING AND WATERING

Keep the compost constantly moist with soft, tepid water and allow the surface to just dry out between waterings. In winter, reduce watering and in low temperatures, keep the compost only slightly moist. In early spring and summer, feed fortnightly with a general houseplant fertilizer. Feed monthly in winter if the plants are in a warm room.

PESTS AND PROBLEMS

If dry air causes browning of the leaf tips, increase humidity and remove badly damaged leaves. Brown patches on the leaves are usually the result of low temperatures or waterlogged compost, so increase temperatures. If no flowers are produced, move the plant to a brighter position.

Check plants regularly - particularly weak specimens - for red spider mites.

LONGEVITY

With appropriate care, spathiphyllums can give you pleasure for many years.

The flower head is made up of the spathe, a large, colourful leaflike structure that enfolds the spadix, which is the true flower cluster.

OTHER VARIETIES OF INTEREST
There are many cultivars and hybrids. The dwarf variety 'Petite' is only 30cm tall. The larger 'Mauna Loa' is more vigorous, growing to 40cm. Although reliable and attractive, it is less hardy and needs warmer winter conditions. Its white, slightly fragrant flowers become pale green with age. *S.* 'Clevelandii' also grows to 40cm.

Below: Spathiphyllum *'Sensation' is a huge plant that can grow up to 90cm tall. It makes a magnificent specimen if you have plenty of space to accommodate it.*

Left: Spathiphyllum *'Cupido'. The gorgeous white flower heads emerge from among deep green leaves in this moderately sized variety.*

Right: *The huge mass of foliage is an ever-present feature of* Spathiphyllum *'Euro-Gigant'. The large, deeply veined leaves are particularly striking.*

STEPHANOTIS

This aristocratic, glossy-leaved evergreen is usually sold trained round a wire hoop, and an almost irresistible, seductive and intoxicating perfume drifts from the clusters of gorgeous star-shaped white flowers. Like many a prima donna, it is sensitive to its surroundings and will only flower in ideal conditions. Spare no effort to ensure that the plant stages a beautiful performance every time.

Stephanotis need constant bright light and warmth; anything less and they will not form flowers. Provide shade in summer from direct sun, which scorches the foliage, and give the plants as much light as possible in winter. They also need constant warmth and are affected by the slightest fluctuations in temperature or cooling draughts. In winter, when watering is reduced, plants will tolerate moderate temperatures. Keep the humidity high, particularly as temperatures increase, by misting regularly with tepid water or by standing plants on a tray of pebbles filled with water to just below the base of the pot. When they become potbound, repot in spring into pots one size larger and water thoroughly. Once they are in a 23 or 25cm pot, topdress each spring by removing and replacing the top 5-7.5cm of compost. Use a peat substitute-based compost. In late winter, carefully unwind the stems from around the hoop and cut back the main stems by half with a pair of sharp secateurs. Remove any weak side shoots and cut the stronger ones back to 7.5cm. When white sap stops oozing from the cuts, tie the stems back into the hoop. Older plants in larger pots can be trained up a tripod of canes, but it will be several years before they reach this stage, as stephanotis can be slow-growing. They also dislike being moved.

As well as Madagascar jasmine, *Stephanotis* is sometimes called wax flower or bridal wreath.

PROPAGATION

Take tip cuttings from non-flowering side shoots in spring or early summer.

1. *Take a healthy 7.5-10cm-long shoot tip from the current year's growth and trim it with a sharp knife just below a leaf joint. Remove the basal leaves.*
2. *Using a pencil or thin cane, make a shallow hole in a 9cm pot of moist cutting compost. If the leaves are large, cut them in half. Dip the base of the cutting in hormone rooting powder, gently tap off the excess. Insert the cutting and firm the compost gently around the stem.*
3. *Place the pot in a loosely knotted plastic bag, supported by canes, and put it in a warm position away from direct light. Once roots are formed and the cutting begins to grow, remove the bag, allow the cutting to acclimatize for about a week and pot it on when the compost is full of roots.*

1

2

3

FEEDING AND WATERING

Use soft, tepid water and keep the compost moist when the plant is actively growing, allowing the surface to dry out between waterings. Reduce watering in winter, keeping the compost just moist, particularly if temperatures are lower, but never allow it to dry out completely.

Feed with a general liquid houseplant fertilizer every two weeks in summer and occasionally in winter; regular feeding is essential for flower production.

PESTS AND PROBLEMS

Prone to scale insect. Check plants regularly for scale, as small infestations are easily controlled, and isolate any affected plants.

Lack of water, fluctuations in temperature and draughts can all cause bud drop.

An absence of flowers, even when the plant is fed, may be the result of low light or temperature fluctuations.

LONGEVITY

Plants that have been well cared for can last many years, particularly if they are grown in a conservatory border.

Below: *If it is happy,* Stephanotis floribunda *produces an abundance of flowers in neat clusters along the stems. Their fragrance is an experience to be savoured.*

Above: *You may see varieties with variegated leaves. They provide year-round colour and interest but you may feel that they distract the eye from the beauty of the flowers.*

Below: *The flowers are of the purest white, and waxy in texture. Remove the flowers as they fade so that the plant puts its energy into producing healthy stem growth.*

Cape primrose

Streptocarpus

It is little wonder that cape primroses are such popular houseplants. Clusters of elegant, trumpet-shaped flowers emerge from dense rosettes of strap-shaped, mid-green leaves. The flowers have intricately veined throats and are produced in shades of white, blue, mauve and pink. Cape primroses will flower throughout the year, but are also happy with a cool winter rest.

To flourish, cape primroses need bright indirect light with protection from summer sunshine, plus moderate temperatures and humidity. They are sensitive to lower temperatures and if it becomes too cool, their response is to stop flowering, restarting when higher temperatures are restored. In summer, when room temperatures increase, or in heated rooms in winter, raise the humidity by standing plants on a shallow tray of pebbles half-filled with water or group several plants together. The usual method of misting is unsuitable, as wetting the leaves easily causes scorching.

Repot annually in spring into shallow pots or pans one size larger than the previous one. Use a peat-substitute compost and water thoroughly with tepid water. To keep the leaves dust-free, gently clean them with a fine, soft paintbrush or a makeup brush and remove any faded flowers and their old stems at the base.

Propagation

Older plants become choked with leaves and flower less freely. However, *Streptocarpus* is easy to propagate.

1 *Select a healthy leaf from the centre of the plant and, using a sharp knife, cut the leaf into 5cm sections with a point at the base.*
2 *Insert the pieces vertically, just deep enough so that they stay upright, into a pot or seed tray containing cutting compost moistened with tepid water. Put four canes in the pot, place the pot in a plastic bag and knot the end. Put it in a bright, warm position away from direct sunshine. If the compost needs rewatering, use a watering can with a long nozzle or place the pot in a container of tepid water and allow it to soak up moisture from below; be sure to let it drain thoroughly. When plants have developed from the small veins at the base and are large enough to handle, pot them singly into 7.5cm pots of peat-substitute mix and pot on as necessary as plants increase in size. Maintain a warm atmosphere until they become established.*

Feeding and watering

Water from below and allow the compost to drain. Let the surface dry out between waterings. At lower winter temperatures, reduce watering, keeping the compost slightly moist. Feed with a liquid flowering houseplant fertilizer every three weeks in summer and once a month in winter. Plants that are resting at lower winter temperatures need no feeding.

Pests and problems

Aphids, mealy bug, mildew.

Leaf tips and margins turn brown in dry air or if there is dryness at the roots; increase humidity and water well with tepid water. Leaf rot at the base is usually caused by overwatering and low temperatures. Remove the rotting leaves and dust with fungicide. Allow the surface of the compost to dry out before rewatering.

If temperatures or light levels are too low, the plant will produce plenty of leaves but no flowers.

Longevity

Plants last a few years before they need propagating.

Left: A cluster of stems bearing violet blue flowers springs from the central rosette of leaves in this fine streptocarpus hybrid.

Right: The glorious rich ruby-red flowers of Streptocarpus 'Neptune' are marked in even deeper tones of red. Several grouped together are a wonderful sight.

Left: Cape primroses can flower from spring through to autumn, so you will have plenty of time to enjoy the delicate flowers of this lovely streptocarpus variety 'Maassens's White'.

OTHER VARIETIES OF INTEREST

Streptocarpus 'Anne': A deep purple, double-flowered cultivar. Very beautiful and distinctive.
S. 'Julie': Upright pale pink flowers with purple markings.
S. 'Kim': A compact, early-flowering variety that produces masses of dark blue flowers.
S. 'Ruby': Masses of rich, deep-red flowers.
S. 'Susan': The flowers are deep magenta with golden yellow throats. A well rounded, compact plant.
S. 'Tina': A free-flowering, compact variety with pale pink upper and magenta lower petals, all distinctly veined.
S. saxorum: A beautiful little species with hairy, fleshy leaves and pale violet flowers on wiry stems.

Goosefoot plant

Syngonium

This wonderful foliage plant produces masses of neat leaves shaped like arrowheads, attractively flushed and patterned in soft, colourful shades. Under ideal growing conditions, these compact bushy plants undergo a transformation in habit and form, becoming vigorous climbers with multilobed leaves, aerial roots and long stems, which can be trained up a moss pole or allowed to trail.

Ideally, the goosefoot plant needs bright light away from direct sunshine all year round, although it will tolerate some shade. Conditions should be constantly moderate to warm, but the plants can withstand slightly lower winter temperatures with careful watering. However, they will not survive if the conditions become too cool. As temperatures increase, they need greater humidity, so group plants together, mist them several times a day with tepid water or stand them on a shallow tray of pebbles filled with water to just below the base of the pot. Wiping the leaves very carefully with a damp cloth not only removes dust but also helps maintain humidity. If the compost is congested with roots, repot plants into a pot one size larger using a peat substitute-based compost. Once the maximum convenient pot size is reached, topdress the plant annually by carefully removing and replacing the top 5cm of compost. Pinch out the growing tips to encourage branching and train the stems up a moss pole. Two or three plants in a pot create the best effect. If plants become straggly, prune them back to within 15-20cm of the base in spring and new stems will regrow. If you wish to retain the arrowhead-shaped leaves and bushy habit, remove the climbing stems immediately they appear.

Propagation

Use tips or stem sections with a leaf for propagation.

1 *Take a healthy 7.5-10cm-long shoot tip from the current season's growth.*
2 *Trim it with a sharp knife just below the leaf joint and remove the basal leaves.*
3 *Using a pencil or thin cane, make several holes a few centimetres deep in a 7.5-10cm pot of moist cutting compost. If the leaves are large, cut them in half. Dip the base of the cutting in hormone rooting powder, gently tapping off the excess. Insert the cutting and firm the compost gently around the stem. Place the pot in a loosely knotted plastic bag, supported by canes, and put it in a warm spot away from direct light. Once roots are formed after four to six weeks and the cuttings begin to grow, remove the bag, water the plants and keep the compost just moist. Allow the cuttings to acclimatize for a week and then pot them into separate containers.*

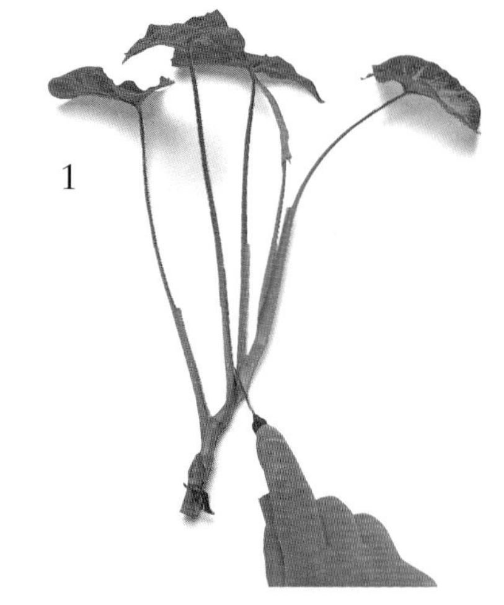

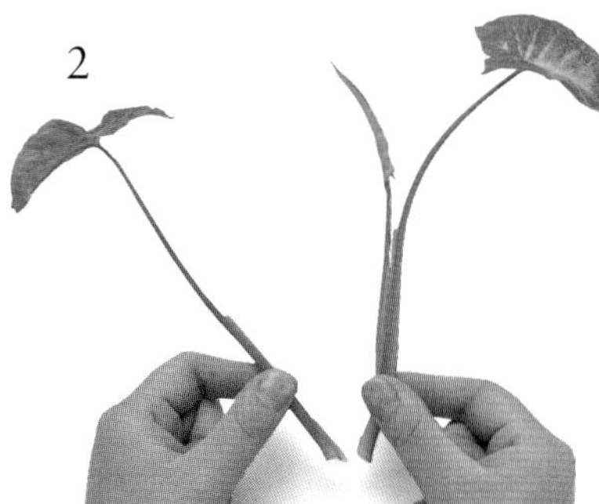

Feeding and watering

Using tepid water, keep the compost moist, allowing the surface to dry out between waterings. This is particularly important in winter if plants are kept at lower temperatures. Feed with a general houseplant fertilizer every two weeks in summer and every four weeks in winter if the plant is not resting and there are signs of growth.

Pests and problems

Scale insect, red spider mite.

Leaves shrivel or become brown and scorched as a result of direct sunshine, dry air or dryness at the roots. Leaf colour fades in low light, so move the plant into a brighter position.

Longevity

Given good growing conditions, syngoniums will last for several years.

Left: S. *'Pixie' makes a compact mound of small leaves when young, but in good conditions it soon becomes a climber.*

Below: S. *'Arrow' has leaves in delicate shades of green, and makes an excellent specimen plant.*

OTHER VARIETIES OF INTEREST
S. 'Maya Red': Pink leaves.
S. podophyllum 'Albovirens': Ivory flushed green leaves with dark margins.
S. p. 'Emerald Gem': Dark green leaves shaded pale green, particularly along veins.
S. p. 'Silver Knight': Silvery green leaves.
S. p. 'Variegatum': Leaves are blotched pale green.
S. p. 'White Butterfly': Silvery green leaves, dark green margins.

Below: S. podophyllum *'Infrared' is aptly named given its extraordinary leaf coloration, perhaps the most unusual of any houseplant.*

TOLMIEA

Tolmieas are tough, attractive, compact plants that produce a mound of bright green, maplelike leaves. Placed outdoors for the summer in a sheltered spot, they often produce spires of tiny, pale, tubular flowers flushed with red. It is the perfect plant for children, who are fascinated by one extraordinary feature, namely the plantlets that appear at the base of the adult leaves.

This is one of the hardiest houseplants; it tolerates cold, draughts, chills, sunshine and shade, but is not particularly fond of hot dry air. Although it will survive in light levels from full sun to shade, it prefers partial shade or bright to medium light. In deep shade, the leaves become pale green and the stalks elongate. It will tolerate a range of temperatures from high to low, and is ideal for unheated rooms kept at just above freezing. It enjoys being outdoors in summer in shelter and shade. Occasional misting with a fine spray of tepid water is a good idea in higher temperatures, and this also encourages plantlets to develop. If the compost becomes congested with roots, repot tolmieas in spring into a pot one size larger, using a peat substitute-based or John Innes No 2 potting compost. Vigorous plants may need repotting twice a year.

PROPAGATION

Tolmieas are very easy to propagate. There is always plenty of material available on a healthy plant

1 Detach leaves with well-developed plantlets.
2 Place them in seed trays or singly in 7.5cm pots of John Innes No 1 or peat substitute cutting compost.
3 Ensure that the stalk is buried and that the plantlet is sitting on the surface of the compost. Keep it moist.

3

Alternatively, peg the plantlets into the compost with a short piece of wire, a hairpin or a small stone and cut the stems from the parent when the plantlets have rooted. The 'mother' leaf may remain green for several months, but when it eventually dries up, remove it carefully from the new plant. As they grow, repot the plants into containers one size larger. Within five or six months, they will have grown to a large and attractive size.

FEEDING AND WATERING

Keep the compost moist when the plants are actively growing and allow the surface to dry out before watering again. Take care not to overwater. In winter, water just enough to prevent the compost from drying out. From spring to autumn, feed every two weeks with a fertilizer for foliage houseplants, but feed only once or twice during winter.

PESTS AND PROBLEMS

Red spider mite can be a problem in a warm dry atmosphere. Check plants regularly, as small infestations are easily controlled, and isolate affected plants.

If the leaf margins turn brown, the atmosphere is too dry and warm. If growth is weak and the foliage pale, move the plant to a brighter position. Limp, shrivelling leaves are a sign of a lack of water or humidity.

LONGEVITY

Repropagate tolmieas regularly. This helps to keep your plants young and vigorous. As houseplants, tolmieas are quite short-lived; they survive longer outdoors.

Left: Tolmiea menziesii *'Taff's Gold' may be labelled as 'Goldsplash', 'Maculata' or 'Variegata'. The irregular mottling on the leaves is unusual yet appealing. It needs bright light for it to be retained.*

Left: *The bright green, hairy leaves of this established* Tolmiea menziesii *tumbling over the edge of the pot are laden with plantlets, fully justifying its common name.*

Right: *Young plantlets form at the base of mature leaves and are easily detached for propagation. A healthy plant should supply you with sufficient material to provide plants for all your friends.*

TRADESCANTIA

Tradescantia fluminensis and its many varieties are grown for their long trailing stems and attractively coloured foliage. Their vigorous growth cascading over the sides of a pot makes them ideal for hanging containers and such is the speed with which the plants develop, that it is not long before they produce a wonderful display. These attractive and easy-to-grow plants are a delight.

Bright light, cool to moderate conditions and adequate humidity are the key to success with *Tradescantia*. Light is important: too much direct sunshine, especially in summer, causes the leaves to bleach or become scorched; too little light and they become green rather than variegated and should be removed. Although constant bright light is preferable, light shade with a few hours of direct sunlight at the beginning or end of the day achieves the same results. Moderate temperatures are ideal, but *Tradescantia* will enjoy a cool position, particularly in winter when it is resting. High humidity is unnecessary at low temperatures, but as it becomes warmer, mist the plants daily in moderate conditions and more often in a centrally heated room, particularly if the plant is growing in a hanging basket. Potgrown plants can stand on moist pebbles in a tray of water filled to just below the base of the pot.

Repot plants each spring for two or three years using a peat substitute-based mixture and then replace them with new cutting material. Stems lose their basal leaves and become straggly, so cut them back in spring to within 5-7.5cm of the base if there are enough leaf joints at the base to provide new growth. Alternatively, thin out older, weaker growth and give the plant good light to encourage it to regrow. Pinch out the growing tips regularly to encourage the lower leaf joints to produce stems, thus making a bushier plant. *Tradescantia* is so easy to propagate that once it ceases to be attractive you can take cuttings. There will be enough on older plants for an ample supply of material.

1

PROPAGATION

Tradescantia is very easy to propagate in spring.

1 *Take healthy 5-10cm stem cuttings. Cut them off cleanly and remove the basal leaves.*

2 *Put the cuttings straight into their final pot filled with potting compost. Hormone rooting powder is not necessary. Use several stems for a better display.*

Cuttings also root easily in water. Once the roots develop, pot the cuttings on, planting two or three in a 7.5cm pot. Take care not to damage the soft, water-filled roots. Pinch out the tips to encourage branching. Varieties with stiffer leaves prefer to be rooted in potting mixture, but are still worth a try in water.

2

FEEDING AND WATERING

Water with tepid water when the plant is growing but do not overwater. Water sparingly in winter at lower temperatures, but more often in warmer rooms. Apply a foliage houseplant feed fortnightly in summer, but only once or twice during the winter months.

PESTS AND PROBLEMS

Aphids may attack soft shoots or flower buds. Red spider mite can be a problem, so check your plants regularly, as small infestations are easier to control.

Shrivelled leaves with brown tips are usually caused by dry air, but check for red spider mite. Carefully cut out any dead growth and mist the plant regularly. If the compost is dry, plunge the pot in a bucket of tepid water for half an hour and then allow it to drain thoroughly.

Limp stems and yellowing leaves are usually the result of plants being underwatered.

LONGEVITY

All the varieties last for several years, but are usually repropagated once they become straggly.

***Left:** Planting several different varieties of* Tradescantia *in a hanging container or pot creates an attractive mixed display and is an interesting alternative to a single variety.*

Above: Tradescantia zebrina *(formerly* Zebrina pendula) *has soft grey-green leaves with a dark central stripe. Pinch out stems for a bushy plant.*

OTHER VARIETIES OF INTEREST

Tradescantia fluminensis 'Albovittata': White striped leaves.
T. f. 'Aurea': Yellow leaves.
T. f. 'Quicksilver': Soft green leaves striped with white.
T. f. 'Tricolor': Striped pink, white and green.
T. pallida: (formerly known as *Setcresea purpurea)*: Unusual rich purple stems and leaves. Coloration is better in bright light. Growth is straggly. Pink flowers appear in summer.

YUCCA

A mature yucca, with its swordlike leaves projecting from thin stems on a stout trunk, is an imposing sight and this, along with a robust nature and tolerance of neglect, ensures its popularity as a houseplant. Coming from the arid areas of central America where rainfall is erratic, it survives direct sunshine, low temperatures, drought and dry air and is the perfect plant for beginners.

Ideally, yuccas should have good light with some direct sunlight all year round; those grown in poor light do not die, but stop growing. From summer to autumn, when there is no danger of frost, they grow happily outdoors, and in winter they prefer cool conditions, although they will survive in a centrally heated room. Yuccas respond well to pruning. In spring, when they become too tall, use a sharp saw to cut back the main stem to the desired height, put the plant in a bright position and new shoots will soon appear. If there are too many shoots and growth becomes congested, remove some and use them as cuttings. Repot smaller plants every other year in spring, using two parts of John Innes No 2 compost to one part of horticultural, or sharp, sand. This mixture and clay pots help to stabilize larger plants. Once a yucca reaches the maximum pot size, topdress it each spring by removing and replacing the top 5cm of compost.

PROPAGATION

In spring, remove offsets or side shoots with 15-23cm leaves from the adult plant using a sharp knife. Pot these into a container of moist, John Innes No 2 compost and stand them in a bright, warm position until they root. Once new growth appears, water them moderately, allowing the surface to dry out before rewatering. Begin feeding after three months.

1 *Alternatively, after pruning, saw the old trunk into 10-13cm sections and seal the top of each piece with wax to prevent water loss. Insert the cutting, unsealed end downwards, into a 7.5-10cm pot of potting mixture, water the compost thoroughly and put the pot in a warm room. This is best done in spring, as the plant will become established during summer.*

2 *Roots and leaves will develop on small stem pieces but will take longer to grow into a decent-sized specimen.*

Right: *Large pieces will also root to create impressive plants.*

FEEDING AND WATERING

Overwatering is the greatest threat to a yucca's survival. Water it sparingly in cool conditions and liberally when the plant is actively growing, allowing the compost surface to dry out between waterings. In the growing season, feed fortnightly with a general houseplant fertilizer and monthly in winter if plants are in a warm room.

PESTS AND PROBLEMS

Yuccas rarely have problems but may suffer from scale. Check them regularly, as smaller infestations are easy to control, and isolate affected plants. Look for clusters of flat, shieldlike scales on stems or leaves, particularly along the veins. If infestations are bad the leaves become sticky. In spring, the active young scale insects, visible through a magnifying glass, can be sprayed with an organic contact houseplant insecticide.

LONGEVITY

Because of their resilience and slow growth, yuccas can live for many years.

OTHER VARIETIES OF INTEREST
Yucca elephantipes 'Variegata' has creamy leaf margins.

Left: *This large specimen of a variegated* Yucca aloifolia *is a stately plant that would grace a spacious room with its elegant simplicity. The impact is increased by planting several stems in one pot. Grouping smaller plants around the base of the pot would be a good way of covering the bare stems.*

Below: Yucca elephantipes *'Jewel' is an attractive variety with sword-shaped leaves suffused with pale yellow stripes and edged in dark green. It makes an excellent specimen plant in the home.*

Above: Yucca elephantipes, *the 'spineless yucca', is widely available and justifiably popular. It has all the attributes of the ideal houseplant: it adds a touch of drama and style to any room, it is resilient and will tolerate considerable neglect, and it is easy to propagate. No wonder it is so popular.*

BROMELIADS

Arguably the ultimate in houseplant design, bromeliads are famous for uniting extraordinary form with outrageous colour. Many of them are more resilient than their appearance suggests and will tolerate cooler conditions. Plants may take between two and ten years to flower, but once the blooms appear, their impact is instant and they can last for many weeks.

All bromeliads grow in shade or partial shade, but some, particularly those with stiff leaves, need bright light to flourish. Bromeliads are usually at their most active in spring and autumn. In winter, if light levels are low and the day length is short, they remain dormant. Bromeliads need constant moderate to warm conditions, although some tillandsias, aechmeas and most stiff-leaved bromeliads survive in lower temperatures, which makes them ideal houseplants.

To maintain constant humidity, stand pots on a shallow tray of pebbles filled with water to just below the base of the pot and mist them occasionally with soft water or rainwater, increasing the regularity as temperatures rise. During summer rain, or if you have soft tapwater, give your plants a quick shower to wash dust from the foliage or wipe them gently with a moist, soft sponge.

Bromeliads need repotting when the compost becomes congested with roots. Use a pot one size larger and a good, free-draining mixture of peat substitute-based potting compost with added orchid compost and grit. If you have the inclination and the facilities, you can make up your own mixture from equal parts of sharp sand or horticultural grit and peat substitute to half a part of leaf-mould. To improve drainage, place a layer of clay pot fragments or aggregate in the bottom of the pot.

Instead of growing bromeliads in pots, try displaying them on 'bromeliad trees' made from driftwood or dead branches. Fill the clefts in the branches with the same mixture as you use for potting, plant the bromeliads and water them in thoroughly.

PROPAGATION

Bromeliads produce offsets at the base of the plant.

1 *When offsets are several months old and at least one third the size of the parent rosette, use an old knife to cut them off. Make sure they have plenty of roots attached.*
2 *Split up clumps of offsets into individual rooted pieces.*
3 *Plant each offset in a pot of the potting compost used for mature plants. Water thoroughly and keep them in moderate to warm conditions. Rewater when the compost dries out, but do not allow water into the leaf rosettes before they root.*

You can also root offsets on creeping stems by covering the stems with potting mix. Sever the offset when roots develop.

FEEDING AND WATERING

Use soft, tepid water to keep the compost moist; with some varieties, the compost should be allowed to dry out completely before rewatering. It is not essential to fill the central 'pool' in bromeliads such as *Aechmea*, but it does help to maintain humidity and provide moisture. At lower temperatures, empty the 'pool' to prevent the water becoming chilled and causing subsequent leaf damage.

From spring to autumn, feed with a liquid fertilizer for flowering houseplants every third watering,

PESTS AND PROBLEMS

Scale and mealy bug sometimes affect bromeliads.

LONGEVITY

Most varieties slowly die after flowering, but because they produce offsets, one original plant can be parent to many healthy offspring.

1

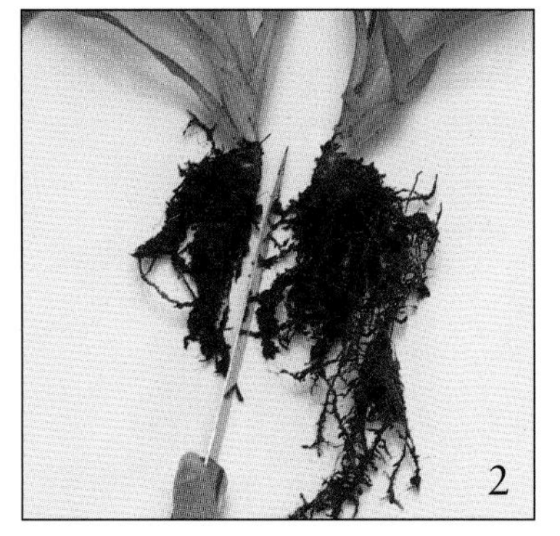

2

3

***Left:** The stunning* Neoregelia *'Tricolor Perfecta' needs good light, watering when the compost is dry and regular feeding with flowering houseplant fertilizer.* Neoregelia meyendorffii *has dark green leaves with a waxy red central area.*

***Above:** The fascinating earth star,* Cryptanthus bivittatus, *is yellow-green in low light, develops a pink tinge in medium light and is vivid pink in bright light.*

***Above:** Although not vital, it is best to keep the central vase full of water, certainly in warm conditions.* Aechmea fasciata *tolerates low humidity and winter cool, but needs bright light. In warmth, it grows all year. Feed the plant in winter.*

Right: Aechmea fasciata, *the urn plant, is easy to grow in pots or on a 'tree'. Beautiful mauve flowers develop in the spiky cluster of pink bracts. It produces offsets on creeping stems.*

OTHER BROMELIADS OF INTEREST

Billbergia: Provide good bright light. The flowers are relatively short-lived. As with *Aechmea*, the plant can spend summer outdoors in partial shade.

Nidularium: Enjoys low light levels and partial shade to shade, and will tolerate cool conditions for short periods. Water when the compost is dry. Continue feeding after flowering. Offsets flower after one or two years.

Below: *The silvery grey-leaved tillandsias are classic air plants. They are often sold attached to sea shells or 'driftwood' for a bathroom display. These can also be 'planted' onto a piece of wood or cork.*

Propagate tillandsias by offsets produced from the stem or basal leaves. When half the size of the parent with a few roots showing, remove the lower leaves of the parent and gently ease out the new plants.

AIR PLANTS

As their name suggests, air plants survive by absorbing water from the atmosphere, using scales that cover the leaf surface, and obtain nutrients from airborne dust. For them to thrive, conditions should be bright, away from direct sunshine, moderate to warm, with good air circulation and, if possible, a humid atmosphere. Mist plants daily with soft, tepid water or rainwater, and in summer add a liquid fertilizer for flowering houseplants at every third watering. Very few kinds survive when grown in pots; they are better grown attached to cork bark or a 'bromeliad tree'. Wrap the base of the plant in sphagnum moss and wind nylon fishing line or plastic-covered wire around the plant to hold it in place. Remove the wire once roots have established.

Left: Guzmania *'Rana' has green-tipped red bracts and soft arching leaves. Other guzmanias include* G. lingulata *with white flowers and brilliant yellow bracts and* G. zahnii *with maroon-tinged, yellow-green leaves, red bracts and vivid yellow flowers.*

Right: Vriesea *'Charlotte' has a long-lasting flower spike and needs light shade and moderate winter conditions.* V. hieroglyphica *has broad, delicately patterned leaves, while* V. splendens *has a fiery orange spike and yellow flowers.*

Left: *The superb variegated form of* Ananas comosus. *It thrives in full sun and eventually becomes too large for a houseplant. In summer, cut off the pineapple, remove the rosette off the top, pare away the flesh, discard the lower leaves, allow it to dry and pot it up.*

Above: Vriesea *'Fire' has a flat swordlike flower head literally aflame with colour and makes a spectacular specimen plant. The foliage and long-lasting flower heads become bleached if light levels are too strong.*

INDOOR BULBS

There is a wonderful range of early-flowering bulbs that are grown to bring spring cheer to the home and after flowering they can be planted outdoors. Many others are tender varieties that can spend summer outdoors but need protection from frost; perhaps the most popular is the *Hippeastrum,* which produces a magnificent floral display during the winter provided it is given a summer rest.

When in flower, *Hippeastrum* needs bright light with moderate temperatures; in higher temperatures the flowers go over quickly. Bulbs are usually on sale in autumn and bloom in winter or spring. When buying, remember that larger bulbs produce more flowers, so choose one which is large and firm. Soak the roots in water for about two hours, then plant the bulb in a well crocked pot of John Innes No 2 compost, leaving the top half to one third of the bulb exposed. Water the bulb a little, keeping the compost slightly moist until signs of growth appear, then gradually increase watering as the bud and flowering stem emerge. Stake the stem for added support if necessary and remove the flowers as they fade. When all the flowers have faded, remove the stem. The appearance of the flowering stem is followed by several broad, straplike leaves and at this stage be sure to feed and water the bulb regularly.

Plants can go outdoors once there is no danger of frost. In midsummer, stop watering so that the leaves turn yellow and die back, then remove the dead leaves. Keep the compost dry for about twelve weeks then begin watering, a little at first and increasingly as more growth appears. Treating them this way ensures that they will flower over winter. It is also possible to continue feeding and watering through the summer, allowing them to rest over winter and encouraging them into growth in spring, to flower in late spring or summer.

Remove and replace the top 2.5cm of compost every year, but as they dislike root disturbance, only repot the plants when the compost becomes congested with roots.

Above: *Use a pot about 2.5cm wider than the bulb and add compost so that the bulb will be half to one third exposed.*

PROPAGATION

Small bulbils appear around the base of the adult *Hippeastrum* bulb. Detach these when they are 2-3cm across, retaining as much root as possible. This is best done at repotting time. Plant young bulbs singly in 7.5cm pots and treat as mature bulbs. *Hippeastrum* can also be grown from seed, but they will take 3-5 years to flower. Do not allow the developing bulbs a resting period.

Above: *Hold the bulb upright and fill in with compost, leaving a gap between the surface and the pot rim for watering.*

FEEDING AND WATERING

Newly potted plants and those that are being encouraged into growth should be watered sparingly at first, increasing the amount as more growth appears. Keep the compost moist when the plant is in active growth. Do not water when the plant is resting. While the leaves are being produced, feed plants fortnightly with a liquid feed for foliage houseplants and when leaf production slows, change to a flowering houseplant fertilizer to encourage the formation of flower buds.

PESTS AND PROBLEMS

Hippeastrum plants are usually free of pests and diseases.

Absence of flowers is usually caused by low light, insufficient watering and irregular feeding with flowering houseplant fertilizer.

LONGEVITY

Hippeastrum bulbs can be kept for many years.

Often, leaves and stems appear together.

Right: Hyacinth *'Blue Delft' is often bought for forcing into flower for an early display. Plant several in a bowl of bulb fibre or a multipurpose compost with the tips protruding.*

Above: Hippeastrum *'Picotee' is a wonderful variety with subtle colour tones. Why not grow it on your windowsill so that passing people can enjoy the exquisite display?*

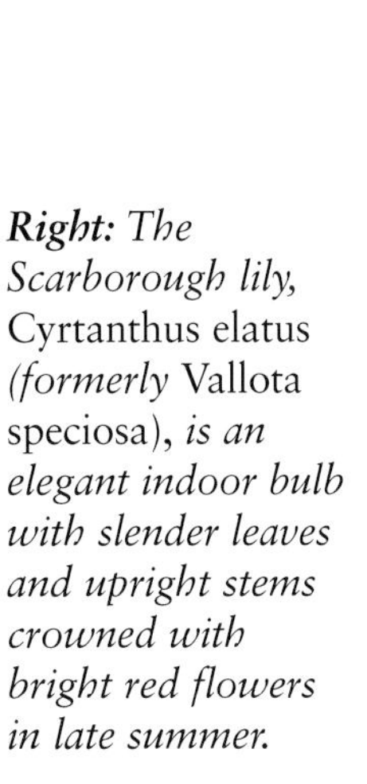

Left: *The* Hippeastrum *bulb shown being planted on page 146 now proudly exhibits its magnificent red-and-white flowers. The variety is 'Minerva'. Stake plants with several large blooms carefully to provide support.*

Right: *The Scarborough lily,* Cyrtanthus elatus *(formerly* Vallota speciosa*), is an elegant indoor bulb with slender leaves and upright stems crowned with bright red flowers in late summer.*

DESERT CACTI

Desert cacti, those great survivors, have a reputation for resilience that regularly leads to their demise, but with a little care and attention they will flourish and flower for decades. Their extraordinary shape and spiny stems are always eye-catching and their flowers are vibrantly coloured and exotic. Some of their rainforest relatives are popular houseplants and the parents of many spectacular flowering hybrids.

Cacti need a bright, sunny position all year; turn them regularly to encourage even growth. In poor light, particularly at high winter temperatures, their stems become elongated and yellow. They survive in a wide range of temperatures, but as houseplants they need moderate conditions during the growing season, with a cool winter rest. They are unaffected by dry air, but appreciate a well-ventilated position, particularly on hot summer days, and can grow outdoors from late summer to early autumn when there is no danger of frost. Repot cacti annually when they are young and in later years only when the compost becomes congested with roots. Late spring is the best time. Use a cacti and succulent compost or John Innes No 1 with added grit or sharp sand, and transfer the plant into a pot one size larger than the previous container. If smooth varieties become dusty, wipe them with a soft damp cloth. Gently spray spiny cacti with tepid water or dust them with an artist's paintbrush.

Cleistocactus strausii

Parodia scopa

Echinopsis chamaecereus

Mammillaria baumii

HANDLE WITH CARE

Wear a pair of thick leather gardening gloves or take a long strip of newspaper and fold it over to make a thick, narrow band of paper 2.5-5cm wide. Wrap this around spiny plants or use a pair of tongs.

FEEDING AND WATERING

From early spring to autumn, when cacti are actively growing, water them with tepid water, allowing the compost surface to dry out before watering again. In winter, at lower temperatures, water plants sparingly only if they begin to shrivel, but more often in higher temperatures. Feed cacti every four weeks during the growing period using a liquid cactus and succulent fertilizer or a liquid fertilizer for flowering houseplants.

Cacti do not flower until they are mature, but you can encourage them to do so by feeding them with a high-potash fertilizer and ensuring they have a cool winter rest.

PESTS AND PROBLEMS

Red spider mite, scale insect and mealy bug can attack cacti.

Overwatering, particularly in cool conditions, causes basal rot. Forgetting to water results in the plant's long, slow demise.

LONGEVITY

In the right position and if well cared for, cacti can survive for decades.

OTHER CACTI OF INTEREST
Rebutia and *Mammillaria* are fun to grow for their vibrant flowers. Also look out for *Ferocactus latispinus*, the fish hook cactus, with its large flat spines, *Ferocactus cylindraceus*, the compass barrel cactus, topped with red spines, and *Astrophytum capricorne*, the goat's horn cactus, covered in twisted spines. Several cacti are clothed in silvery hairs, such as *Cephalocereus senilis*, old man cactus, while others in orange or red are grafted onto green stems and look like lollipops.

PROPAGATION
Divide and pot up clump-producing cacti, such as *Mammillaria, Gymnocalycium* and *Echinopsis* in late spring or early summer.

1 *Remove the compost from around the larger offsets. Sever the offsets, dust the cuts with fungicide and leave them for a few days for a callus to form.*
2 *Plant the offsets in a small pot of cactus potting compost, add a shallow layer of washed grit and label.*

FOREST CACTI

Although we usually associate cacti with desert conditions, some of the most popular cultivars grown as houseplants have their origins in the tropical rainforests of Central and South America, where they grow in the clefts and branches of trees. Their long, often trailing stems make a wonderful display in hanging baskets or pots on a tall plinth and the vibrantly coloured flowers are a joy to behold.

PROPAGATION

1 *Select a healthy undamaged stem and remove two or three 'pads' by pulling firmly where the segments join. Allow the 'raw' end to dry out for a few hours so that a callus forms over it.*

2 *Fill a 9cm pot with peat substitute-based compost and insert four pieces deep enough for them to stay upright. Place them in a warm bright place and water sparingly when the compost is dry. Rooting powder and plastic bags are not necessary.*

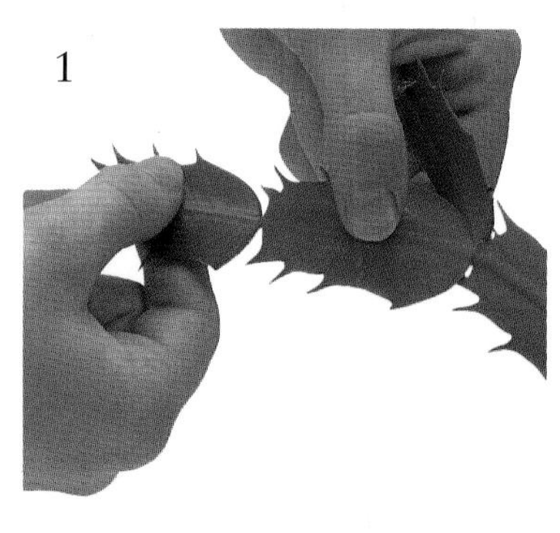

Forest cacti need good light away from direct sunshine and are happiest at moderate temperatures, with cool conditions when resting. Unlike their desert cousins, they appreciate humidity and are ideal for a bathroom; mist them regularly with soft tepid water or stand plants on a tray of pebbles filled with water to just below the base of the pot. If the compost has become congested with roots, repot plants into a pot one size larger in spring, using a mixture of two parts peat-substitute compost to one part sharp sand or perlite.

Schlumbergera hybrids, commonly known as Christmas cactus, need moderate to warm conditions for much of the year. They flower in winter, after which they need about eight weeks rest in a cool room, keeping the compost moderately moist and allowing the surface to dry out before rewatering. When the resting period is over, move the plant to a moderately warm room. Once the danger of frost has passed, it can spend the summer outdoors in a partially shaded position. Keep the compost moist but make sure that it does not become waterlogged by summer rain. Feed every two weeks with a liquid fertilizer for flowering plants or tomato fertilizer from late spring until the flower buds appear. In late summer or early autumn, bring the plant indoors into a cool room and water it when the surface of the compost is dry. Flower bud formation is stimulated by a reduction in daylight hours, so keep plants in a spare room, away from artificial light. As soon as the buds start to form, move the plant into its display position in moderate temperatures and leave it there until flowering is over. Moving plants in bud causes bud drop, so once you have chosen their display position, do not move or turn the plants. Once flowering is over, the plants need a resting period and the annual cycle then begins again.

Hatiora gaertneri (Rhipsalidopsis gaertneri), the Easter cactus, needs similar treatment to *Schlumbergera,* but the flowering period is from mid- to late spring. After flowering, treat it as for *Schlumbergera* until the flower buds form in mid-spring, then move the plant into its display position in a moderate room, keeping the compost moist. After flowering, you can put the plant outdoors and the cycle begins again. Propagate after flowering, using the method shown for *Schlumbergera* on this page.

FEEDING AND WATERING

Use soft, tepid water and keep the compost moist after flowering until the resting period. At this point, allow the compost surface to dry out between waterings. After the resting period, when the buds begin to form, water when the compost surface just begins to dry out. Keep the compost moist when in flower and feed with a liquid fertilizer suitable for flowering plants every two weeks until after flowering.

PEST AND PROBLEMS

Mealy bug may affect forest cacti. Overwatering causes them to rot. Slugs can be a problem for those spending the summer outdoors.

LONGEVITY

Forest cacti will live for many years and develop into wonderful specimens.

***Right:** The* Schlumbergera *hybrids, or Christmas cactus, are justifiably popular for the masses of flowers they produce at a time when there is little in bloom, either indoors or out.*

ORCHID CACTUS

Epiphyllum, the orchid cactus, needs similar treatment to the Easter cactus, but flowers in late spring to early summer. Many epiphyllums have magnificent, fragrant, saucer-shaped blooms. After flowering, put the plant outdoors. In early autumn, bring it into a room at moderate temperatures and water when the compost surface starts to dry out. In early winter, move it into a cool room and water when the compost surface has dried out. In early to late spring when flower buds appear, move the plant to its display position in a moderate room and keep the compost moist. Once the plant has finished flowering, the cycle begins again.

Hybridizing Schlumbergera *has now produced a huge range of flower colours.*

Above: Epiphyllum *'Pegasus' has huge dazzling pink flowers with pale margins. With such spectacular blooms, it is little wonder that it is also known as the orchid cactus.*

Right: *When the blooms appear, the dull green Easter cactus,* Rhipsalidopsis, *becomes a magnificent specimen plant.*

Right: Epiphyllum *'Queen Anne' has magnificent pale yellow and cream flowers. Such delicate tints show the remarkable range of colours to be found among these cacti.*

FERNS

For an elegant display of the finest foliage, ferns are unbeatable. Their seductive beauty has beguiled houseplant lovers for decades. Many ferns have young fronds like a bishop's crozier that slowly unfurl to exhibit their fresh lush growth. Some survive at low light levels, others at low temperatures, but nearly all kinds dislike dry compost or air, making them ideal plants for the bathroom or kitchen.

Most ferns like moderate to bright light, away from scorching sunshine, and although many tolerate low light levels for a short time, it is unsuitable for long-term growth. As with all houseplants, turning them every two or three days ensures balanced growth from all round the plant. Ferns enjoy moderate to warm conditions, although many are able to tolerate lower temperatures with careful watering. At lower temperatures, ferns from warmer climates stop growing, but soon start again when temperatures rise. Dry air causes browning of the leaves, so constant humidity is vital, particularly at higher temperatures; mist plants regularly with soft tepid water, group several plants together or stand them on trays of moist pebbles half-filled with water.

Spring or early summer is repotting time, but only when the pot is congested with roots or the rhizomes have spread over the sides. Use a pot one size larger and a peat-substitute compost and water well. Once a fern has reached maturity and the maximum pot size, divide or repot it in fresh compost every two to three years.

Left: Splitting up Adiantum.

PROPAGATION

Divide the crown in spring by removing the fern from its container and carefully teasing off the potting compost. Cut the rhizome into pieces, each with at least one healthy growing point. Plant into small pots of moist, peat-substitute compost and enclose them in a plastic bag for about four weeks in a warm, shaded position. Water sparingly at first, then move plants to their new position and treat as mature specimens.

Some ferns are propagated by the spores on the underside of the fronds. Remove a whole frond or part of one and put it on a sheet of white paper or in a paper bag. When the dustlike spores are shed, fill a 9cm pot with peat-substitute compost and firm the surface. Stand the pot in a tray of water for an hour before allowing it to drain or water it using a watering can with a rose. Scatter the spores over the surface. Stand the pot in a saucer of water and cover it with a plastic bag or clingfilm. Refill the saucer as required. Place the pot in a warm bright spot. When new plants appear after several months, remove the clingfilm and pot on.

FEEDING AND WATERING

Keep the compost constantly moist but not waterlogged; if ferns dry out they soon die. If possible, use soft tepid water. When plants are actively growing, feed them every two weeks with a general liquid fertilizer. During winter or at lower temperatures, stop feeding them.

PESTS AND PROBLEMS

Scale, mealy bug and aphids may attack ferns. Many ferns are damaged by insecticides, so read the label carefully. It is safer to use alternative forms of control. Squash aphids or wash them off with a weak detergent solution and remove mealy bug and scale by dabbing them with an artist's paintbrush or cotton bud dipped in methylated or surgical spirits.

Browning tips and yellowing fronds are signs of dry air. Excessive sunshine causes pale fronds and scorching. If growth is weak and fronds are pale green, increase feeding or decrease watering.

LONGEVITY

With the correct care, ferns can last for very many years.

Left: Adiantum bicolor *has neat overlapping 'leaflets' on thin dark stems and needs moist, warm, shady conditions to thrive.*

Left: *Provide cool to moderate conditions for* Adiantum capillus-veneris, *which is highly susceptible to dry air and dry compost.*

Above: Platycerium bifurcatur, *the stag's horn fern, grows on cork bark or in a pot. It prefers moderate temperatures, but can tolerate coolness for short periods.*

Right: Asplenium nidus, *the bird's nest fern, needs shade and humidity. Remove dust by supporting the fronds gently and wiping them with a damp sponge.*

Right: Nephrolepis exaltata *'Dallas Jewel' is one of the many different types of sword fern, the most well known being the Boston fern. They flourish in bright light, in moderate to warm conditions, and a well-grown plant looks truly magnificent.*

Left: Pteris cretica *'Albolineata' needs moderate to warm conditions and good light. Compact, it is ideal for small spaces.*

Below: Blechnum gibbum, *dwarf tree fern, develops a stout trunk topped by glossy, feathery leaves.*

Left: *The button fern,* Pellaea rotundifolia, *is a pretty little plant with almost circular 'leaflets'. It needs constant moderate temperatures and light to thrive.*

Below: Dryopteris erythrosora *has beautiful brick red young growths. An ideal fern for cool shade.*

Left: *The round clusters on the leaf undersides of* Cyrtomium falcatum *contain ripening spores - not scale insects!*

Below: *The popular holly fern,* Cyrtomium falcatum, *is unique among indoor ferns in that it tolerates dry air, draughts and light levels ranging from shade to bright light, with some sun.*

Left: Didymochlaena truncatula *produces attractive deep bronze young growths that mature to a deep glossy green. An excellent fern for a shady position.*

PALMS

With their arching fans or feathery fonds, palms lend a dignified air of elegance to any room. Such bold architectural foliage makes them ideal as specimen plants, standing isolated for their glory to be appreciated. They thrive in moderate to cool conditions and hate overwatering or disturbance at the roots. If they are well cared for, these slow-growing plants can last for many years.

Most palms thrive in bright light, away from direct sunshine, and although they will survive at lower light levels, growth is usually poor. If you only have room for a palm in a shady spot, moving it into bright light for a few hours each day or a week every month certainly encourages healthier growth. Palms need constant, moderate temperatures, away from draughts. They dislike high temperatures, so ensure that warm rooms are well ventilated in summer. If your house is centrally heated, it is better to move palms to a cool spare room in winter. Most palms grown as houseplants are happy to spend summer outdoors in partial shade, away from the effects of scorching sunshine, but remember to bring them indoors before the first frosts. Mist plants regularly, using soft, tepid water if possible or stand smaller specimens on trays of pebbles filled with water to just below the base of the pot.

Palms dislike root disturbance, so only repot them when they are heavily potbound. Use a pot one size larger and place a 2.5cm layer of pea gravel or broken pot fragments in the bottom of the pot to improve drainage. Use John Innes No 2 compost with added peat substitute or leaf-mould, and firm the compost, layer by layer as you fill the pot, leaving at least 2.5cm of space between the rim and compost level for watering. Potting large palms into wooden half barrels or clay pots gives them extra stability; plastic pots are fine for smaller specimens.

Summer rain washes dust from the leaves of palms standing outdoors, but you can also clean plants by gently spraying them under the shower or by wiping the leaves with a sponge moistened with tepid water.

PROPAGATION

Palms can be grown from seed, but may take up to two or more years to germinate. Place them in a peat-substitute compost, label the seed and keep them warm and moist.

Some palms produce offsets that can be detached from the parent in spring, using a sharp knife. Pot them up into a 1:1 compost mix of peat substitute and sharp sand or perlite. Water the offsets thoroughly with tepid water and allow them to drain. Enclose the pot in a loosely knotted plastic bag and stand it in bright indirect or filtered light in a constantly warm position. Water just enough to prevent the compost from drying out. Rooting may take up to three months. Once the plant begins to grow, remove the bag and begin watering, sparingly at first. As the plant becomes established, feed it with a general liquid houseplant fertilizer once every four weeks. It can be repotted the following spring.

***Left:** Palm seeds vary in size and shape. The date palm,* Phoenix dactylifera, *can be planted from a fruit stone.*

FEEDING AND WATERING

Water palms thoroughly and do not rewater them until the compost surface has dried out. Keep the compost slightly moist in winter. With smaller palms, you can plunge the pot into a container of tepid water for about an hour and then allow the compost to drain. If possible, use soft water or rainwater. Palms hate to be overwatered; it makes the leaves turn brown and rot. If this happens, remove the affected parts, stop watering and rewater when the compost surface is almost dry. Feed palms every two weeks when they are actively growing, with a general houseplant fertilizer.

PESTS AND PROBLEMS

Scale, red spider mite and mealy bug may affect palms.

Brown leaf tips are caused by dry or cold air, overfeeding or underwatering. Cold draughts, overwatering or underwatering may cause leaves to turn yellow. Brown spots on the leaves are caused by chilling or overwatering. Lower leaves turn brown and die as part of their natural cycle. Cut them off carefully with a sharp knife or scissors.

Above: Lytocaryum weddellianum, *usually labelled* Microcoelum weddellianum, *is grown for its elegant feathery fronds. It appreciates humidity and shade. Repot it with care, as it is sensitive to root damage.*

Left: Caryota mitis *is one of the most beautiful palms and the shape of the leaflets gives the plant its common name of the fishtail palm. It grows well in poor light.*

Right: The parlour palm, Chamaedorea elegans, *tolerates low light, dry air and neglect. Mature plants are particularly handsome.*

Left: Cocos nucifera *is not the easiest palm to grow at home. It needs high temperatures and humidity and is usually short-lived.*

The new palm sprouts from the 'coconut' at the base.

Left: Howea forsteriana, *the majestic Kentia palm, has graceful arching fronds and dark green leaflets. It thrives in low light but dislikes any dryness at the roots.*

Right: Phoenix canariensis, *the Canary Island date palm, can be grown as an indoor plant during its early years, but eventually becomes unmanageable in the home. It needs bright light to succeed.*

Right: *When buying palms for the house, remember that although they are small initially, some grow to an enormous size. This young* Ravenea rivularis, *the majesty palm, can eventually reach a truly majestic 12m in height!*

Right: Chrysalidocarpus lutescens, *the areca palm, is an elegant clump-forming plant with green-and-gold stems. They must have bright light, warmth and high humidity to thrive.*

SUCCULENTS

All cacti are succulents, but not all succulents are cacti. Succulents are specialized plants that appear in many different plant groups. They are able to store water in their stems and leaves, which often leads to their downfall as watering is frequently neglected. In summer, they need regular watering, but at cooler winter temperatures only occasional watering is needed; given this treatment they will flourish.

As you would expect, succulents appreciate a position on a bright, sunny, well-ventilated windowsill. Provide moderate to warm conditions in the growing season; succulents are perfectly happy outdoors from late spring to early autumn when there is no danger of frost. The leaves of some varieties are covered with white 'powder' and these types need protection from the rain. In winter, succulents do better in a cool room, although higher temperatures are acceptable. Repot your plants every two to three years into a cacti and succulent compost or John Innes No 1 with added sharp sand, perlite or horticultural grit. Ease the plant from the pot by turning it upside down and pushing a pencil through each of the drainage holes. If the compost is congested with roots or clump-forming succulents have spread to the rim of the pot, repot them into a container one size larger or repropagate them. Otherwise, tease away the old compost from the roots, wash the existing pot and put a good layer of clay crocks in the base for drainage. Fill it with new compost. Plant clump-forming succulents in half pots or pans and trailing types in hanging baskets or pots.

Below: Succulents come in a multitude of form, habit, leaf shapes and sizes and are ideal plant for children's rooms.

FEEDING AND WATERING
From spring to autumn, water succulents thoroughly with tepid water when the compost surface has dried out. In winter, in cooler conditions, give them a little water if they show signs of wilting. Water them more often at higher temperatures. Water them from above or stand the pot in a shallow tray of water until the compost surface is moist and darkens. Allow it to drain thoroughly. Succulents in plastic pots need less watering than those in clay pots. When they are actively growing, feed them every month with a cacti and succulent fertilizer or a general liquid one. Slow-growing succulents do not need feeding.

LONGEVITY
With care, succulents can last many years.

PESTS AND PROBLEMS
Mealy bug. Over watering causes rot. Flower only when mature, helped by feeding and a cool winter rest.

PROPAGATION

Leaf cuttings can be taken all year round, but are better done in spring as growth starts.

1 *Carefully pull or cut a few leaves from the base of the plant. Dust the wounds with a fungicide and allow a callus to form on the cuttings. This may take two or three days in spring or summer and several weeks in winter.*
2 *Fill a 7.5cm pot with cactus potting compost, stand the cuttings on top and firm them in. Fill the pot with washed horticultural grit, label it and place it in a moderately warm, partially shaded position. Keep the compost slightly moist.*
3 *When new plants appear, separate and pot them into individual pots. Many of the leaf succulents are propagated like this, including* Gasteria and Haworthia.

It is also possible to propagate succulents from stem cuttings or by dividing and potting up offsets from clump-producing kinds.

OTHER VARIETIES OF INTEREST

Garden centres and specialist nurseries stock a huge variety of plants. Look out for *Ceropegia woodii,* the rosary vine, with trailing stems and heart-shaped leaves; *Lithops*, the living stones; *Kalanchoe tomentosa,* with grey, woolly, brown-tipped leaves; *Sedum morganianum*, the trailing, grey-green-leaved donkey's tail; *Senecio rowleyanus,* the string of beads, with globular leaves.

TEMPORARY DISPLAYS

There are countless plants that will provide an attractive, temporary floral display in the home. Many last for several weeks or even months; some can even be grown for a few years, but most are inexpensive and usually discarded after flowering. For a good show, protect them from high temperatures and remove fading flowers regularly. Otherwise they require very little maintenance and are excellent value for money.

***Below:** There is a huge range of* Senecio cruentus, *or cineraria, hybrids and they are deservedly popular for their masses of brightly coloured flowers. They flourish in cool conditions and moist compost, but take care not to overwater them. Stand plants on a tray of pebbles filled with water to just below the base of the pot.*

***Right:** Hybrids of* Eustoma grandiflorum, *the prairie gentian, make very pretty flowering plants. They need a bright position with some sunshine, moderate to warm conditions and regular misting. Avoid overwatering and allow the compost surface to dry out between waterings.*

Below: Gerbera jamesonii, *the brightly coloured Barbeton daisy, likes moderate to warm conditions and bright light with some morning or afternoon sun. Keep the compost moist and mist plants occasionally. When they finish flowering, plants can be discarded or grown on. Water them sparingly in winter, divide the crown and repot them in spring.*

Below: *There are many compact cultivars of* Browallia speciosa, *a good value houseplant with starlike flowers. Under good conditions, the flowers last for many weeks. It likes cool conditions, bright light, moist compost and occasional misting. Feed it every two weeks with a flowering houseplant fertilizer and remove the dead flowers regularly.*

There is a wide range of varieties and colours of primroses, such as the Primula vulgaris (shown right) *or the beautiful* Primula obconica (shown above). *This plant, although attractive, can cause an allergic skin rash. Cool bright conditions and moist compost with regular misting will keep primroses healthy. After flowering, plant them outdoors in dappled shade.*

Left: *When you buy* Exacum affine, *the beautiful Arabian violet, make sure it has plenty of buds and some flowers. Keep it in cool bright, draught-free conditions with moist compost, and mist it regularly or stand it on a tray of pebbles filled with water to just below the base of the pot. Deadhead frequently for a longer flowering period.*

Below: Catharanthus roseus, *the Madagascar periwinkle, looks very much like a busy Lizzie, with forms in white and pink. It needs bright light with some sunshine, moderate temperatures, moist compost and occasional misting. This good value plant flowers from spring to autumn.*

Above: Dendranthema *x* grandiflorum *varieties, the pot chrysanthemum, likes moderate temperatures, good light and occasional misting. Keep the compost moist and deadhead regularly for a floral display that will last about two months. You can plant them outdoors after flowering.*

Left: *The white form of Madagascar periwinkle,* Catharanthus roseus *'Albus', is a pretty plant with a tiny cerise central spot on the flowers. The blooms stand out well displayed against a dark background. Deadhead regularly to encourage further flowering.*

PESTS AND DISEASES

Do not be discouraged - you are not alone! Even the most experienced houseplant enthusiast has problems with pests and diseases. Organic, chemical or cultural - there are many methods of control, but well-cared-for plants are always more likely to survive. Vigilance is paramount: check your plants as often as possible and remember that isolation and early treatment limit the damage and ensure rapid control.

APHIDS

Aphids (right) appear in clusters, spreading rapidly and attacking soft sappy growth or flower buds. Look for sticky patches on the leaves and white, shed skins littering the plant. Heavy infestations cause weak, distorted growth. Small populations can be squashed by hand, sprayed with soft soap or tackled with an organic houseplant insecticide.

MEALY BUGS

Mealy bugs (below) are small, grey crawling insects covered with a white mealy powder and waxy threads. They weaken plants by sucking the sap. Remove light infestations with a damp cloth, fine paintbrush or cottonbud dipped in surgical or methylated spirits. Treat with a systemic houseplant insecticide. Quarantine new plants for several weeks if possible, to avoid introducing pests to your collection.

SCALE INSECT

Clusters of flat, shieldlike scales (above) may appear on stems or leaves, particularly along the veins and midrib. The leaves become sticky. Wipe off the scale insects with a damp cloth, sponge or a cottonbud dipped in soapy water. Alternatively, dab off the insects using an artist's paintbrush dipped in methylated or surgical spirits. Spray the plant with a systemic houseplant insecticide. In spring, you can spray the active young, visible through a magnifying glass, with an organic houseplant insecticide.

Whitefly
Signs of infestation are yellowing and stickiness of the leaves and black mould forming on them. Gently brushing the leaves causes clouds of small flies to appear, from the undersides of the leaves where they are usually found (below). Spray them with an organic houseplant insecticide, such as pyrethrum. As this only deals with the adult whiteflies, you will need to spray the plants regularly, outdoors if it is warm.

Red spider mite
Red spider mites flourish where the air is hot and dry. They are very small and difficult to see; look for speckling and mottling on the leaf surface (above) and bronzing of the leaves, particularly at the top of plants. In the later stages, fine webbing appears on leaves and stems, punctuated by tiny, translucent orange dots. Weak plants are more likely to be attacked. Control the mites by spraying them regularly with derris or any organic houseplant insecticide. Increase humidity. In severe cases, prune away the affected areas and spray, or dispose of the plant completely.

Grey mould
Grey mould (above) can be a problem if plants are overwatered, when water is left on soft or hairy leaves, or if a plant is kept in cool, damp conditions. Remove the affected parts and any surrounding debris with a sharp knife, increase the temperature, improve air circulation and spray or dust with fungicide.

Powdery mildew
Powdery mildew (below) eventually causes leaf drop. Improve air circulation, and spray with fungicide. Plants that are dry at the roots for long periods are more susceptible. Before using any treatments, read manufacturers' instructions and plant care labels.

PLANT INDEX

Page numbers in **bold** indicate major text references. Page numbers in *italics* indicate captions and annotations to photographs. Other text entries are shown in normal type.

A

B

C

CREDITS

The majority of the photographs featured in this book have been taken by Neil Sutherland and are © Colour Library Books. The publishers wish to thank the following photographers for providing additional photographs, credited here by page number and position on the page, i.e. (B)Bottom, (T)Top, (C)Centre, (BL)Bottom left, etc.

Pat Brindley: 35(BL), 91(TR), 93(TR), 111(TL), 141(BL)
John Glover: 18, 48, 49(BR), 91(BR), 97(TR), 151(TC,TR), 155(TR,CR)
Holt Studios International:
170(BC), 171(BL): Duncan Smith, 171(TL,TR,BR): Nigel Cattlin
Harry Smith Photographic Collection: 170(R)
S & O Mathews: 93(BR)
Photos Horticultural: 83(BL), 141(BR), 151(BR)

Author's acknowledgments

The author would like to thank Roy Lancaster and David Linnell. Thanks are also due to Gill Biggs for her invaluable support, to Neil Sutherland for his photographic skill and good humour and to everyone at Ideas into Print for their patience, enthusiasm and encouragement.

Publisher's acknowledgments

The publishers would like to thank Philip Sonneville nv, Lochristi, Belgium and The Flower Auction Holland, Naaldwijk for providing high-quality plants and photographic facilities for the preparation of this book.

Thanks are also due to: Boonwood Garden Centre, Brockings Exotics, BVBA Gebr. Hellebuyck Hub. & Fern., Chessington Nurseries, Country Gardens at Chichester, Dibley's Nurseries, Hawley Garden Centre, Hills Nurseries, Holly Gate Cactus Nursery, Kaktuskwekery Ariane, Kwekerij Mariënoord b.v., Millbrook Garden Centre, Murrells Nursery and The Palm Centre.